Underage Drinking

Other books in the Issues That Concern You series:

ISSUES THAT CONCERN YOU

Underage Drinking

Noël Merino, *Book Editor*

Christine Nasso, *Publisher*
Elizabeth Des Chenes, *Managing Editor*

GREENHAVEN PRESS
A part of Gale, Cengage Learning

GALE
CENGAGE Learning™

Detroit • New York • San Francisco • New Haven, Conn • Waterville, Maine • London

© 2008 Gale, Cengage Learning

For more information, contact
Greenhaven Press
27500 Drake Rd.
Farmington Hills, MI 48331-3535
Or you can visit our Internet site at gale.cengage.com

ISBN-13: 978-0-7377-3091-3
ISBN-10: 0-7377-3091-9
Library of Congress Control Number: 2007939018

Printed in the United States of America
3 4 5 6 7 12 11 10 09 08

CONTENTS

INTRODUCTION

The National Minimum Drinking Age Act of 1984 requires all states to have the age of twenty-one as the minimum age allowed to legally purchase and publicly possess alcohol. Any state that does not adhere to the act faces a reduction of its state highway funds. As of 2007, all states were in compliance with the act. The drinking age act specifically requires states to prohibit the "purchase and public possession" of alcoholic beverages to those under the age of twenty-one, but does not require prohibition of drinking alcoholic beverages by those under the age of twenty-one in every circumstance. The term *public possession* is strictly defined and has the following exceptions: for an established religious purpose; when accompanied by a parent, spouse, or legal guardian age twenty-one or older; for medical purposes when prescribed or administered by a licensed physician, pharmacist, dentist, nurse, hospital, or medical institution; in private clubs or establishments; and the sale, handling, transport, or service in dispensing of alcoholic beverage pursuant to lawful employment of a person under the age of twenty-one by a duly licensed manufacturer, wholesaler, or retailer of alcoholic beverages.

While most people would agree that alcohol should not be publicly available to minors of a certain age, the appropriate drinking age is still debated.

Currently, the minimum age to vote and to serve in the military in the United States is eighteen. Many believe that if a person is old enough to vote and serve in the military, then he or she should be treated like an adult and trusted with the responsibility to determine whether or not to consume alcohol. Others argue that setting the drinking age at twenty-one saves society from a number of harms committed by younger drinkers. This sentiment is expressed by Mothers Against Drunk Driving, which notes, "Like it or not, it is clear that more young people were killed on the highways when the drinking age was 18."

At a staged car crash in Independence, Ohio, local high-school students watch as emergency workers and their classmates act out the consequences of drunk driving.

Often those who do not agree with the drinking age law simply ignore it. In many cases, adults of drinking age play a role in facilitating underage drinking by buying alcohol, selling alcohol, or allowing those under twenty-one to drink in their house. While the law prohibits the purchase and public possession of alcohol by those under twenty-one in every state, each state's laws vary widely regarding the legality of private possession and consumption of alcohol by those under twenty-one. State laws also vary regarding adults who furnish alcohol to minors.

While the law in almost half of the states allows parents to legally furnish alcohol to their own underage children, it does not necessarily allow adults to furnish alcohol to other underage individuals. Nonetheless, many parents have decided to allow drinking in the home by their underage children and others. Parents who have hosted parties for teenagers argue that teens drink alcohol at parties no matter where they are held, so allowing drinking at home cuts down on the dangers to their kids and others. Virginia resident Elisa Kelly threw a party for her son's sixteenth birthday and allowed alcohol at the party. She is now serving a twenty-seven-month sentence in jail for providing alcohol to minors. "No one was hurt. No one drove anywhere. I really don't think I deserve to go to jail for this long," Kelly noted, stating that she was motivated by a desire to keep the kids safe. "I've seen too many photographs of teenagers being killed in car wrecks because of drinking and driving."

On the other side of the debate, many people echo the sentiment of Joseph Califano Jr., chairman and president of the National Center on Addiction and Substance Abuse at Columbia University. Califano believes that the best way to stop underage drinking lies with parents, causing him to call prevention "a mom and pop operation." To deter parents from allowing their underage children and others to drink and to eliminate the exceptions to the law in some states, local governments around the country are enacting statutes that make it a misdemeanor for people to knowingly allow minors to consume alcohol at parties hosted at private residences. Violation of these statutes, known as "social host ordinances," can lead to fines, jail time, and can make the party host liable for injuries sustained by third parties as a result of any minor guest's negligence.

Is the minimum age set too high at twenty-one? Should parents be allowed to decide whether or not to allow their child to drink at home, regardless of their age? What are the risks of underage drinking? How can underage drinking be prevented? These issues are among the topics discussed in the following chapters. The chapter titled "What You Should Know About Underage Drinking" offers crucial facts about drinking and its impact on young people, and the chapter "What You Should Do About Underage Drinking" offers tips to young people who may confront the issue in their own lives. This book also includes a list of suggestions for further reading and a list of organizations to contact for more information. With all of these features, *Issues That Concern You: Underage Drinking* is an excellent resource for those interested in exploring this issue.

ONE

Causes, Risks, and Prevention of Underage Drinking

National Institute on Alcohol Abuse and Alcoholism

> In the following article, authored by the National Institute on Alcohol Abuse and Alcoholism (NIAAA), some of the causes of underage drinking, the risks of underage drinking, and prevention strategies for underage drinking are discussed. The NIAAA, part of the U.S. Department of Health & Human Services, provides leadership in the national effort to reduce alcohol-related problems. Alcohol is the drug of choice among youth. Many young people are experiencing the consequences of drinking too much, at too early an age. As a result, underage drinking is a leading public health problem in this country.

Each year, approximately 5,000 young people under the age of 21 die as a result of underage drinking; this includes about 1,900 deaths from motor vehicle crashes, 1,600 as a result of homicides, 300 from suicide, as well as hundreds from other injuries such as falls, burns, and drownings.

Yet drinking continues to be widespread among adolescents, as shown by nationwide surveys as well as studies in smaller populations. According to data from the 2005 Monitoring the Future (MTF) study, an annual survey of U.S. youth, three-fourths of 12th graders, more than two-thirds of 10th graders, and about

National Institute on Alcohol Abuse and Alcoholism (NIAAA), "Underage Drinking: Why Do Adolescents Drink, What Are the Risks, and How Can Underage Drinking Be Prevented?" January 2006.

two in every five 8th graders have consumed alcohol. And when youth drink they tend to drink intensively, often consuming four to five drinks at one time. MTF data show that 11 percent of 8th graders, 22 percent of 10th graders, and 29 percent of 12th graders had engaged in heavy episodic (or "binge") drinking within the past two weeks [January 2006].

Research also shows that many adolescents start to drink at very young ages. In 2003, the average age of first use of alcohol was about 14, compared to about 17½ in 1965. People who reported starting to drink before the age of 15 were four times more likely to also report meeting the criteria for alcohol dependence at some point in their lives. In fact, new research shows that the serious drinking problems (including what is called alcoholism) typically associated with middle age actually begin to appear much earlier, during young adulthood and even adolescence.

Other research shows that the younger children and adolescents are when they start to drink, the more likely they will be to engage in behaviors that harm themselves and others. For example, frequent binge drinkers (nearly 1 million high school students nationwide) are more likely to engage in risky behaviors, including using other drugs such as marijuana and cocaine, having sex with six or more partners, and earning grades that are mostly Ds and Fs in school.

Why Some Adolescents Drink

As children move from adolescence to young adulthood, they encounter dramatic physical, emotional, and lifestyle changes. Developmental transitions, such as puberty and increasing independence, have been associated with alcohol use. So in a sense, just being an adolescent may be a key risk factor not only for starting to drink but also for drinking dangerously.

Risk-Taking—Research shows the brain keeps developing well into the twenties, during which time it continues to establish important communication connections and further refines its function. Scientists believe that this lengthy developmental period may help explain some of the behavior which is characteristic of adolescence—such as their propensity to seek out new and potentially dangerous situations. For some teens, thrill-seeking might include experimenting with alcohol. Developmental changes also offer a possible physiological explanation for why teens act so impulsively, often not recognizing that their actions—such as drinking—have consequences.

Expectancies—How people view alcohol and its effects also influences their drinking behavior, including whether they begin to drink and how much. An adolescent who expects drinking to be a pleasurable experience is more likely to drink than one who does not. An important area of alcohol research is focusing on how expectancy influences drinking patterns from childhood through adolescence and into young adulthood. Beliefs about alcohol are established very early in life, even before the child begins elementary school. Before age 9, children generally view alcohol negatively and see drinking as bad, with adverse effects. By about age 13, however, their expectancies shift, becoming more positive. As would be expected, adolescents who drink the most also place the greatest emphasis on the positive and arousing effects of alcohol.

Sensitivity and Tolerance to Alcohol—Differences between the adult brain and the brain of the maturing adolescent also may help to explain why many young drinkers are able to consume much larger amounts of alcohol than adults before experiencing the negative consequences of drinking, such as drowsiness, lack of coordination, and withdrawal/hangover effects. This unusual tolerance may help to explain the high rates of binge drinking among young adults. At the same time, adolescents appear to be particularly sensitive to the positive effects of drinking, such as feeling more at ease in social situations, and young people may drink more than adults because of these positive social experiences.

Personality Characteristics and Psychiatric Comorbidity—Children who begin to drink at a very early age (before age 12) often share similar personality characteristics that may make them more likely to start drinking. Young people who are disruptive, hyperactive, and aggressive—often referred to as having conduct problems or being antisocial—as well as those who are depressed, withdrawn, or anxious, may be at greatest risk for alcohol problems. Other behavior problems associated with alcohol use include rebelliousness, difficulty avoiding harm or harmful situations, and a host of other traits seen in young people who act out without regard for rules or the feelings of others (i.e., disinhibition).

The Role of Genetics and Environment

Hereditary Factors—Some of the behavioral and physiological factors that converge to increase or decrease a person's risk for alcohol problems, including tolerance to alcohol's effects, may be directly linked to genetics. For example, being a child of an alcoholic or having several alcoholic family members places a person at greater risk for alcohol problems. Children of alcoholics (COAs) are between 4 and 10 times more likely to become alcoholics themselves than are children who have no close relatives with alcoholism. COAs also are more likely to begin drinking at a young age and to progress to drinking problems more quickly.

Research shows that COAs may have subtle brain differences which could be markers for developing later alcohol problems. For example, using high-tech brain-imaging techniques, scientists have found that COAs have a distinctive feature in one brainwave pattern (called a P300 response) that could be a marker for later alcoholism risk. Researchers also are investigating other brainwave differences in COAs that may be present long before they begin to drink, including brainwave activity recorded during sleep as well as changes in brain structure and function.

Some studies suggest that these brain differences may be particularly evident in people who also have certain behavioral traits, such as signs of conduct disorder, antisocial personality disorder, sensation-seeking, or poor impulse control. Studying how the brain's structure and function translates to behavior will help researchers to better understand how predrinking risk factors shape later alcohol use. For example, does a person who is depressed drink to alleviate his or her depression, or does drinking lead to changes in his brain that result in feelings of depression?

Students on spring break in 2004 gather and cheer as one young woman drinks beer through a funnel.

Other hereditary factors likely will become evident as scientists work to identify the actual genes involved in addiction. By analyzing the genetic makeup of people and families with alcohol dependence, researchers have found specific regions on chromosomes that correlate with a risk for alcoholism. Candidate genes for alcoholism risk also have been associated with those regions. The goal now is to further refine regions for which a specific gene has not yet been identified and then determine how those genes interact with other genes and gene products as well as with the environment to result in alcohol dependence. Further research also should shed light on the extent to which the same or different genes contribute to alcohol problems, both in adults and in adolescents.

Environmental Aspects—Pinpointing a genetic contribution will not tell the whole story, however, as drinking behavior reflects a complex interplay between inherited and environmental factors, the implications of which are only beginning to be explored in adolescents. And what influences drinking at one age may not have the same impact at another. Genetic factors appear to have more influence on adolescent drinking behavior in late adolescence than in mid-adolescence.

Environmental factors, such as the influence of parents and peers, also play a role in alcohol use. For example, parents who drink more and who view drinking favorably may have children who drink more, and an adolescent girl with an older or adult boyfriend is more likely to use alcohol and other drugs and to engage in delinquent behaviors.

Researchers are examining other environmental influences as well, such as the impact of the media. Today alcohol is widely available and aggressively promoted through television, radio, billboards, and the Internet. Researchers are studying how young people react to these advertisements. In a study of 3rd, 6th, and 9th graders, those who found alcohol ads desirable were more likely to view drinking positively and to want to purchase products with alcohol logos. Research is mixed, however, on whether these positive views of alcohol actually lead to underage drinking.

The Health Risks of Alcohol

Whatever it is that leads adolescents to begin drinking, once they start they face a number of potential health risks. Although the severe health problems associated with harmful alcohol use are not as common in adolescents as they are in adults, studies show that young people who drink heavily may put themselves at risk for a range of potential health problems.

Brain Effects—Scientists currently are examining just how alcohol affects the developing brain, but it's a difficult task. Subtle changes in the brain may be difficult to detect but still have a significant impact on long-term thinking and memory skills. Add to this the fact that adolescent brains are still maturing, and the study of alcohol's effects becomes even more complex. Research has shown that animals fed alcohol during this critical developmental stage continue to show long-lasting impairment from alcohol as they age. It's simply not known how alcohol will affect the long-term memory and learning skills of people who began drinking heavily as adolescents.

Liver Effects—Elevated liver enzymes, indicating some degree of liver damage, have been found in some adolescents who drink alcohol. Young drinkers who are overweight or obese showed elevated liver enzymes even with only moderate levels of drinking.

Growth and Endocrine Effects—In both males and females, puberty is a period associated with marked hormonal changes, including increases in the sex hormones, estrogen and testosterone. These hormones, in turn, increase production of other hormones and growth factors, which are vital for normal organ development. Drinking alcohol during this period of rapid growth and development (i.e., prior to or during puberty) may upset the critical hormonal balance necessary for normal development of organs, muscles, and bones. Studies in animals also show that consuming alcohol during puberty adversely affects the maturation of the reproductive system. . . .

Preventing Underage Drinking

Intervention approaches typically fall into two distinct categories: (1) environmental-level interventions, which seek to reduce opportunities for underage drinking, increase penalties for violating minimum legal drinking age (MLDA) and other alcohol use laws, and reduce community tolerance for alcohol use by youth;

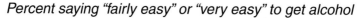

Availability of Alcohol Among Eighth, Tenth, and Twelfth Graders

Percent saying "fairly easy" or "very easy" to get alcohol

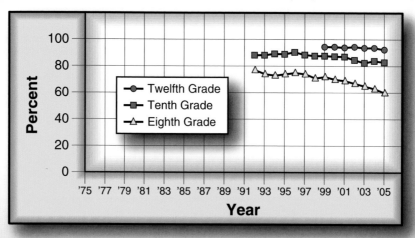

Taken from: National Institute on Drug Abuse, *Monitoring the Future: National Results on Adolescent Drug Use, 2005.*

and (2) individual-level interventions, which seek to change knowledge, expectancies, attitudes, intentions, motivation, and skills so that youth are better able to resist the pro-drinking influences and opportunities that surround them.

Environmental approaches include:

Raising the Price of Alcohol—A substantial body of research has shown that higher prices or taxes on alcoholic beverages are associated with lower levels of alcohol consumption and alcohol-related problems, especially in young people.

Increasing the Minimum Legal Drinking Age—Today all States have set the minimum legal drinking at age 21. Increasing the age at which people can legally purchase and drink alcohol has been the most successful intervention to date in reducing drinking and alcohol-related crashes among people under age 21. NHTSA [National Highway Traffic and Safety Administration] estimates that a legal drinking age of 21 saves 700 to 1,000 lives annually. Since 1976, these laws have prevented more than 21,000 traffic deaths. Just how much the legal drinking age relates to drinking-related crashes is shown by a recent study in New Zealand. Six years ago that country lowered its minimum legal drinking age to 18. Since then, alcohol-related crashes have risen 12 percent among 18- to 19-year-olds and 14 percent among 15- to 17-year-olds. Clearly a higher minimum drinking age can help to reduce crashes and save lives, especially in very young drivers.

Enacting Zero-Tolerance Laws—All States have zero-tolerance laws that make it illegal for people under age 21 to drive after *any* drinking. When the first eight States to adopt zero-tolerance laws were compared with nearby States without such laws, the zero-tolerance States showed a 21-percent greater decline in the proportion of single-vehicle night-time fatal crashes involving drivers under 21, the type of crash most likely to involve alcohol.

Stepping up Enforcement of Laws—Despite their demonstrated benefits, legal drinking age and zero-tolerance laws generally have not been vigorously enforced. Alcohol purchase laws aimed at sellers and buyers also can be effective, but resources must be made available for enforcing these laws.

Individual-Focused Intervention

School-Based Prevention Programs—The first school-based prevention programs were primarily informational and often used scare tactics; it was assumed that if youth understood the dangers of alcohol use, they would choose not to drink. These programs were ineffective. Today, better programs are available and often have a number of elements in common: They follow social influence models and include setting norms, addressing social pressures to drink, and teaching resistance skills. These programs also offer interactive and developmentally appropriate information, include peer-led components, and provide teacher training.

Family-Based Prevention Programs—Parents' ability to influence whether their children is well documented and is consistent across racial/ethnic groups. Setting clear rules against drinking, consistently enforcing those rules, and monitoring the child's behavior all help to reduce the likelihood of underage drinking. The Iowa Strengthening Families Program (ISFP), delivered when students were in grade 6, is a program that has shown long-lasting preventive effects on alcohol use. . . .

Underage Drinking Is Dangerous

Today, alcohol is widely available and aggressively promoted throughout society. And alcohol use continues to be regarded, by many people, as a normal part of growing up. Yet underage drinking is dangerous, not only for the drinker but also for society, as evident by the number of alcohol-involved motor vehicle crashes, homicides, suicides, and other injuries.

People who begin drinking early in life run the risk of developing serious alcohol problems, including alcoholism, later in life. They also are at greater risk for a variety of adverse consequences, including risky sexual activity and poor performance in school. Identifying adolescents at greatest risk can help stop problems before they develop.

TWO

Exaggerating the Problem of Underage Drinking Is Ineffective Prevention

David J. Hanson

In the following article, David J. Hanson, professor emeritus of sociology at the State University of New York at Potsdam, argues that the problems of underage drinking have been overstated and distorted in an attempt to scare young people from drinking. Hanson also argues that these attempts have been unsuccessful and the very real problem of alcohol abuse needs to be addressed. He claims that a better solution is to teach young people responsible use of alcohol. Hanson has received alcohol-research grants from federal and state agencies, has numerous publications on the topic of alcohol, and hosts a Web site dedicated to the topic.

Alcohol abuse is a significant problem among young people and a solution needs to be found. This [article] evaluates prevention programs and identifies effective and ineffective ways to reduce drinking problems among young people, especially high school, college, and university students. The best preventive measures are often the easiest and most economical and can be easily implemented by parents and educators.

David J. Hanson, "Underage Drinking," *Alcohol: Problems and Solutions*, alcoholinformation.org, April 2007. Reproduced by permission.

Distorted Statistics

We've all seen the distressing headlines. Case in point—newspapers across the country carried frightening statistics reported by Joe Califano and the Center on Addiction and Substance Abuse (CASA).

On national television programs, Califano reported horror stories of alcohol abuse among college students, associating it with assault, rape, and even murder. A CASA report asserted that:

- "60 percent of college women who have acquired sexually transmitted diseases, including AIDS and genital herpes, were under the influence of alcohol at the time they had intercourse"
- "90 percent of all reported campus rapes occur when alcohol is being used by either the assailant or the victim"
- "The number of women who reported drinking to get drunk more than tripled between 1977 and 1993"
- "95 percent of violent crime on campus is alcohol-related"

But relax. These assertions are not supported by the facts. According to an investigative reporter, one of these statistics "appears to have been pulled from thin air," another is based on no evidence whatsoever, another is based on one inadequate survey and is inconsistent with all other surveys, and a fourth is highly suspect at best.

Even the most improbable of statistics are often repeated by news media as fact and become part of public belief. It is now commonly believed that the average young person will have seen 100,000 beer commercials between the age of two and eighteen But just think—sixteen years or about 5,844 days occur between a person's second and eighteenth birthday. To see 100,000 beer commercials in that period, a person would have to see an average of more than seventeen a day! Common sense alone should have been enough to dispel the myth. But this clearly absurd statistic has been gullibly repeated over and over:

- by the Center for Science in the Public Interest in the *New York Times*
- in *Sports Illustrated*

- in Congressional testimony by Senator Strom Thurmond, the National Council on Alcoholism, and The Center for Children
- by Remove Intoxicated Drivers (RID) on "Sonya Live"
- by former Surgeon General Everett Koop in the *New York Times*
- and in countless newspapers and magazines across the country

This blatantly erroneous statistic has even found its way into textbooks for students and in materials for teachers.

The Reason for Distorted Statistics

Distorted, biased, or incorrect statistics may attract media attention. They may even influence public policy. But they can't contribute to a reduction of alcohol abuse, which requires accurate information and unbiased interpretation. Therefore, we must be skeptical of surprising, sensationalized statistics.

Typically, inflated statistics are associated with talk of epidemics, threats to our youth, and similar alarmist language. Often they are promoted by groups with laudable sounding names such as the Center for Science in the Public Interest. But many such groups, which may have underlying social or political agendas, tend to exaggerate the extent and growth of problems in which they have a vested interest and, typically, a proposed solution. Problems widely seen by the public as being of epidemic proportion justify ever larger budgets, increased staffs, higher salaries, more power, and greater organizational prestige.

And many groups and individuals have a vested interest in exaggerating the extent of drinking problems. They generally include federal, state, and other governmental alcohol agencies; private alcohol agencies; alcohol treatment facilities, therapists, alcohol educators; and often alcohol abusers themselves.

Editors sometimes confess that sensational statistics have much more reader appeal than reports of generally declining problems. Thus, when alcohol statistics are presented by researchers, the media tend to spin stories in a negative light. For example, the *Wall Street Journal* ran the following headline and lead sentence

Alcohol Use Among 12- to 17-Year-Olds in 2005

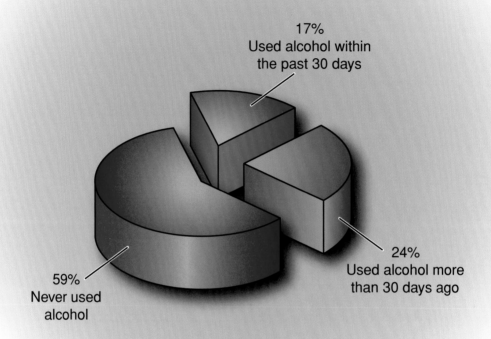

17%
Used alcohol within
the past 30 days

24%
Used alcohol more
than 30 days ago

59%
Never used
alcohol

Taken from: U.S. Department of Health and Human Services, Substance Abuse and
Mental Health Services Administration, Office of Applied Studies. National
Survey of Drug Use and Health, 2005.

in response to a press release by the Harvard School of Public
Health:

"BINGE" DRINKING AT NATION'S COLLEGES IS
WIDESPREAD, A HARVARD STUDY FINDS

BOSTON—Almost half of all students surveyed at 140 U.S.
colleges admitted to "binge" drinking, leading to everything
from fights to vandalism according to . . .

Instead, the study could have resulted in this headline and lead story:

MAJORITY OF COLLEGE STUDENTS DRINK MODERATELY OR NOT AT ALL, A HARVARD STUDY FINDS

BOSTON—More than half of all students surveyed at 140 U.S. colleges report moderate drinking as the campus norm, resulting in relatively small numbers (only 9 percent) who get hurt or vandalize according to . . .

Similarly, a nation-wide survey of students at 168 U.S. colleges and universities found that:

- 98% have never been in trouble with a college administrator because of behavior resulting from drinking too much
- 93% have never received a lower grade because of drinking too much
- 93% have never come to class after having had several drinks
- 90% have never damaged property, pulled a false alarm, or engaged in similar inappropriate behavior because of drinking

The Real Statistics: College Students

While headlines typically express alarm over drinking epidemics among collegians, in reality drinking among college students continues to decline as abstaining from alcohol climbs:

- The proportion of college students who abstain from alcohol jumped 58% between 1983 and 1994, according to a series of nation-wide surveys
- A 16% increase in college non-drinkers has been found between the periods of 1989–1991 and 1995–1997 by the federally-funded CORE Institute
- A recent study by Dr. Henry Wechsler of Harvard University found that the proportion of collegiate abstainers in the U.S. jumped nearly 22% in the four years since his earlier study

- The proportion of non-drinkers among college students in the U.S. recently reached a record-breaking all-time high according to statistics collected for the National Institute on Drug Abuse by the Institute for Social Research of the University of Michigan. That means that *the proportion of students who drink has dropped to an all-time record-breaking low!*
- The proportion of first year college students who drink beer has fallen dramatically and recently reached the lowest level in 30 years, according to national annual surveys by UCLA's Higher Education Research Institute. Similar drops were found for wine and distilled spirits.

So-called binge drinking among American college students also continues to decline For example, the proportion of college students who binge decreased significantly within a recent four-year period, according to the Harvard University study mentioned above.

These findings are consistent with data collected for the National Institute on Drug Abuse by the Institute for Social Research [ISR]. The ISR found that *college "binge" drinking in the U.S. recently reached the lowest level* of the entire 17-year period that its surveys have been conducted.

College students "simply don't drink as much as everyone seems to think they do," according to researchers who used Breathalizers at the University of North Carolina at Chapel Hill. Even on the traditional party nights of Thursday, Friday and Saturday, 66% of the students returned home with absolutely *no* blood alcohol content; two of every three students had not a trace of alcohol in their systems at the end of party nights.

"I'm not surprised at all by these results," said Rob Foss, manager of Alcohol Studies for the UNC Highway Traffic Safety Center, which conducted the study with funding from the National Highway Traffic Safety Administration and the North Carolina Governor's Highway Safety Program. "Other Breathalizer studies we have done with drivers and recreational boaters show similar results—less drinking than is generally believed. We have substantial misperceptions about alcohol use in this country."

The Real Statistics: Teenagers

Similarly, drinking among young people in general continues to decline. For example, the proportion of youths aged 12 through 17 who consumed any alcohol within the previous month has dropped from 50% in 1979 down to 19% in 1998, according to the federal government's *National Household Survey on Drug Abuse*. That's down from one of every two youths to fewer than one of every five.

The proportion of both junior and senior high school students who have consumed any alcohol during the year has dropped again for the third year in a row, according to the PRIDE Survey, a nation-wide study of 138,079 students, which is designated by

In an attempt to teach responsible drinking habits, Colby College serves alcohol in its dining halls to students—like these women—who are age 21 or older.

federal law as an official measure of substance use by teenagers in the U.S.

Within a period of 17 years, there has been a 13% decrease in the proportion of American high school seniors who have ever consumed alcohol and a 24% *decrease in the proportion who have ever "binged."*

These are very important facts, but you probably haven't seen or heard much, if anything, about them in the mass media.

Exaggeration Fuels the Problem

In spite of all the hype and exaggeration, the fact remains that alcohol abuse is still a significant problem among youth that requires our attention. Thus, the question remains: what can we do to reduce alcohol abuse?

Significantly, hype and exaggeration are actually an important part of the problem. A negative spin on drinking statistics has a negative impact on drinking behaviors by contributing to a "reign of error." When people believe that "everyone is doing it," abusive drinking increases as they try to conform to the imagined behaviors of others. This is especially true among young people. Perceptions of the drinking behaviors of others strongly influences the actual drinking behavior of students.

The exaggeration of alcohol abuse tends to create a self-fulfilling prophesy. The more young people believe heavy drinking occurs, the more heavily they tend to drink in order to conform. Research has demonstrated that reducing misperceptions of alcohol abuse is an effective way to reduce actual abuse among adolescents.

Individual students almost always believe that most others on campus drink more heavily than they do and the disparity between the perceived and the actual behaviors tends to be quite large. By conducting surveys of actual behavior and publicizing the results, the extent of heavy drinking can be quickly and significantly reduced. The most carefully assessed such project demonstrated a 35% reduction in heavy drinking, a 31% reduction in alcohol-related injuries to self, and a 54% reduction in alcohol-related injuries to others.

This approach to reducing alcohol problems is remarkably quick and inexpensive and has proven to be highly effective.

Cultural Examples of Successful Moderation

Alcohol is a part of Western society and the majority of Americans enjoy alcohol beverages. To pretend that young people will grow up to enter a world of abstinence is both unrealistic and irresponsible.

Even religious groups strongly committed to abstinence are not very successful in maintaining it among their young people, the majority of whom drink. This is true even among students attending church supported schools. Why should we expect secular alcohol education to even reach that very low level of "success"? It can't—and it won't.

But many groups around the world have learned how to consume alcohol widely with almost no problems. Those familiar to most Americans include Italians, Jews, and Greeks. The success of such groups has three parts: 1) beliefs about the substance of alcohol, 2) the act of drinking, and 3) education about drinking.

In these successful groups:

- The substance of alcohol is seen as neutral. It is neither a terrible poison nor is it a magic substance that can transform people into what they would like to be
- The act of drinking is seen as natural and normal. While there is little or no social pressure to drink, there is absolutely no tolerance for abusive drinking
- Education about alcohol starts early and starts in the home. Young people are taught—through their parents' good example and under their supervision—that if they drink, they must do so moderately and responsibly

This three-part approach has enabled many groups to avoid the alcohol abuse problems that have plagued our society. Yet our federal government and others in the U.S. prevention field fail to learn from the experience of successful groups, opting instead to portray alcohol as a "dirty drug" to be feared and avoided; to promote abstinence as the best choice for all people; and to work toward reducing all, including moderate and responsible, consumption of alcohol beverages.

The Current Strategy: Scare Tactics

Federal agencies systematically attempt to equate legal alcohol consumption with illegal drug use. For example, federal guidelines direct agencies to substitute "alcohol and drug use" with "alcohol and other drug use" and to avoid use of the term "responsible drinking" altogether. Alcohol is also stigmatized by associating it with crack cocaine and other illegal drugs. A poster picturing a wine cooler warns "Don't be fooled. This is a drug."

Technically, this assertion is correct. Any substance—salt, vitamins, water, food, etc.—that alters the functioning of the body is a drug. But the word "drug" has negative connotations and the attempt is clearly to stigmatize a legal product that is used in moderation by most American adults.

Stigmatizing alcohol as a "drug" may trivialize the use of illegal drugs and thereby encourage their use. Or, especially among the very young, may create the false impression that parents who use alcohol in moderation are drug abusers whose good example should be rejected by their children. Thus, this misguided effort to equate alcohol with illicit drugs is likely to be counterproductive.

The Solution: Teaching Responsible Use

Instead of stigmatizing alcohol and trying to scare people into abstinence, we need to recognize that it is not alcohol itself but rather the abuse of alcohol that is the problem.

Teaching about responsible use does not require student consumption of alcohol any more than teaching them world geography requires them to visit Nepal, or teaching them civics requires that they run for office or vote in presidential elections. We teach students civics to prepare them for the day when they can vote and assume other civic responsibilities if they choose to do so.

Because either drinking in moderation or abstaining should both be equally acceptable options for adults, we must prepare students for either choice. To do otherwise is both irresponsible and ineffective, if not counterproductive.

A recent study of the effectiveness of alcohol education programs compared those that present an abstinence-only message with those that present drinking in moderation as an option. It is clear that programs accepting responsible use are demonstrably more successful than are no-use-only programs.

In spite of noble intentions and the expenditure of massive amounts of time, energy, and money the best evidence shows that our current abstinence-oriented alcohol education is ineffective. Simply doing more of what is not working will not lead to success; it is essential that we re-think our approach to the problem. Our youth are too important and the stakes are too high to do otherwise.

THREE

Underage Drinkers Often Binge on Alcohol

Julie Mehta

> In the following article, Julie Mehta discusses one of the biggest worries about underage drinking: binge drinking. She interviews several teens who have experienced binge drinking. These teens discuss the negative impacts that binge drinking had on their lives, including unwanted pregnancy, blacking out, and a near-death experience. Julie Mehta is a writer in New York City.

The last thing Sebastien remembers about the fall weekend in 2003 when he and his friends visited a state college for a football game was drinking a half-gallon of whiskey. "When I woke up, I thought I was dead because all I saw was a bright white light," the 18-year-old from Nashville, Tenn., recalled. "Then I realized I was in the hospital. The paramedics had found me lying facedown on the side of the road. I'd flatlined [in the ambulance] on the way to the hospital, but they brought me back."

The high school senior from Tennessee had a blood alcohol concentration (BAC) of 0.42 percent, more than five times the state level of legal drunkenness (0.08 percent). BAC is the amount of alcohol present in the blood, and it increases exponentially with each drink a person consumes.

Julie Mehta, "Wasted: Life's No Party for Teens Who Drink Too Much, Too Fast," *Current Health 2*, vol. 31, issue 6, February 2005, pp. 15-18. Reproduced by permission.

Sebastien discovered the hard way one of the frightening consequences of binge drinking (drinking with the intention of becoming drunk). Those consequences can also include stunted brain development and car accidents.

Problem Drinkers

The good news is that teens aren't drinking as much as people might think. According to a survey by the U.S. Centers for Disease Control and Prevention, 80 percent of eighth graders and more than half of 12th graders had not drunk any alcohol in the 30 days preceding the survey.

The bad news is that among those who had consumed alcohol, most drank too much, too fast. "The pattern among teen drinkers

Ball State University students at an off-campus party play a drinking game. Binge drinking like this is not uncommon among college students.

is an average of six drinks at a time, six times a month, while for adults it's three drinks at a time, eight times a month," Susan Foster, director of policy research for the National Center on Addiction and Substance Abuse at Columbia University in New York, explained to *Current Health*. "So binge drinking is more the norm among young people." According to national surveys, about 30 percent of all high school seniors and 12 percent of all eighth graders binge-drink in a given two-week period.

Defining Binge Drinking

Binge drinking—not to be confused with alcoholism (a progressive addiction to alcohol that interferes with daily life)—is a style of drinking generally defined as having five or more drinks in a row for men and four or more drinks in a row for women. "That's how much would make the typical adult [legally drunk], but teens aren't fully grown, so it takes less for them to get impaired," said Vivian Faden, an epidemilogist with the National Institute on Alcohol Abuse and Alcoholism (NIAAA). Epidemiology is a branch of medicine that deals with the incidence, spread, and control of diseases.

Other factors influence how alcohol affects a person, including genetics, food consumption, and, most important, the person's weight and gender. "A female's ability to metabolize alcohol at the gut level is less, so if you take a male and female student, both 120 pounds, the female will have a higher BAC with the same number of drinks," explained Ralph Lopez, an adolescent medicine specialist in New York City.

Taking Things to Extremes

The disparity in the effect of alcohol on boys versus girls isn't the only gender difference. Experts say that the reasons boys and girls tend to drink also vary. "With boys, drinking is usually about sensation seeking and having fun," said Foster. "With girls, it's more about coping with negative emotions and relieving anxiety or depression."

Jessica from Spokane, Wash., was in the sixth grade when she binged for the first time while staying overnight at a friend's house. She and her friend pulled a bottle of tequila from the liquor cabinet and drank it with orange juice. "At first I didn't like it, but after a while, it felt normal. It was the first time in my life I felt complete," Jessica told *CH* [*Current Health 2* magazine].

The next day, she had a horrible hangover and promised herself not to drink again. But she did—at first a few times a month, then once a week, having four drinks at a time on average. Jessica started

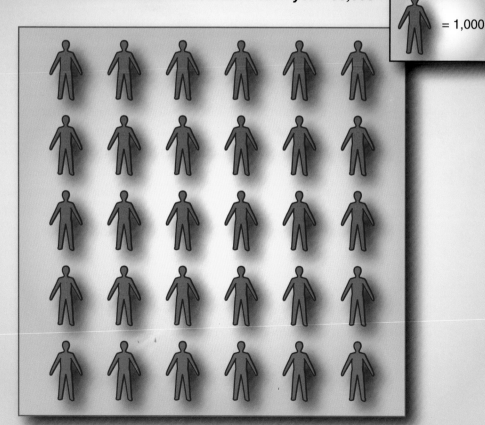

One of the Big Risks of Underage Drinking Is Binge Drinking

Number of college students who require emergency treatment for alcohol overdose each year: 30,000

= 1,000

Taken from: American College of Emergency Physicians

drinking with older boys and found herself getting more and more intoxicated trying to keep up with their drinking pace.

"Teens are at a place in their development where they will take things to extremes," said Andrew Finch, director of the Association of Recovery Schools, a group of high schools scattered across the country for teens overcoming substance abuse problems. "They're testing their limits, and they feel invincible."

Chase from Concord, Calif., started drinking at age 11. "I would drink alcohol at parties," he said. "I felt like I fit in, and I didn't worry about the consequences." Soon he found he needed more booze to get drunk and started blacking out, forgetting what had happened while he was drinking. "I would wake up with cuts from falling down the stairs and getting into fights I didn't remember," he said.

Hitting Bottom

Initially, people who drink alcohol may feel that they're "loosening up," said Finch. "But before you know it, you lose your handle on reality and do things you wouldn't usually do."

For 16-year-old Ty from Spokane, Wash., alcohol became an obsession. "If someone said, 'Let's get drunk tonight,' that's all I could think about all day," he said. He stopped spending time with his siblings and started stealing cars with his friends. Finally he was caught and sent to an alcohol abuse rehabilitation program.

Chase was caught with booze repeatedly before being ordered into a long-term treatment program. Now 16, he admits, "I lost a lot of trust with my mom and little brother, and I lost my self-respect."

For some teens, the consequences of drinking, especially bingeing, can be much worse. Researchers estimate that it is a factor in one- to two-thirds of sexual-assault and date-rape cases among teens and college students. A study by the Kaiser Family Foundation showed that 23 percent of sexually active teens and young adults in the United States had unprotected sex because they were drinking or using drugs at the time. Failure to use a condom can lead to transmission of diseases such as HIV. In

Jessica's case, it led to her getting pregnant at age 14. She stopped drinking and got treatment before giving birth to a girl last May.

Dead Drunk

You have probably heard plenty about the dangers of drinking and driving, but that's not the only way booze kills. "Alcohol is the leading contributor to death among youth under 21," said Faden. Each year, 7,000 young people die because of alcohol-related accidents, including drowning and motor-vehicle crashes. Another 1,800 lose their lives through murders or suicides in which alcohol played a role.

Even if you make it home safely after drinking, a nasty hang-over may not be your only worry. "Alcohol is a respiratory and central nervous system suppressant," said Lopez. At first, alcohol stimulates the brain, but with each additional drink, the brain progressively slows down. "At 0.10 percent BAC, a fair number [of people] will show inebriation. At 0.20, very few will not have some impairment of abilities. Once you're above 0.30, you're lucky you're still breathing. At 0.40, you and the Grim Reaper are walk-ing hand in hand."

That's why Sebastien, with a 0.42 BAC that autumn night, was so lucky to survive. Each year, hundreds of people die of an alcohol overdose, many of them college students. Some choke on their own vomit while passed out. In others, the areas of the brain that control life functions simply shut down. For months before he nearly died, Sebastien had been drinking 12 to 15 beers several times a week. Now a college freshman, he is surrounded by more temptation. However, Sebastien says, drinking is no longer an option. "I knew I'd be dead by 19 if I didn't stop."

This Is Your Brain on Alcohol

Even a few hours of binge drinking can have far-ranging effects. "The brain continues to develop into the early 20s, and exposing the brain to alcohol in that period may impair brain develop-ment," Faden said. Several studies have shown that alcohol can have lingering effects on the hippocampus, an area of the brain used for learning and memory. "It gets out of control," said Jessica. "Things happen you can't change."

"Looking back now, I think drinking was a waste of my time," said Chase. "Life is a lot richer being clean."

FOUR

The Drinking Age Laws Must Be Enforced to Stop Underage Drinking

Rebecca Kanable

In the following article, Rebecca Kanable explores enforcement of drinking age laws. Kanable discusses several strategies for reducing underage drinking, including changing attitudes, compliance checks, shoulder tap campaigns, keg registration laws, education, and other solutions. Rebecca Kanable is a writer who regularly publishes on the topic of law enforcement.

High school students sit around a bonfire drinking beer. Young college students gather at a house known for loud drinking parties. A very young-looking person walks out of a liquor store with a tall bottle disguised in a brown paper bag.

If you come across any of these things happening in your community, what do you do? And, after finding out what your reaction was, how will your community react? If you enforce the law, will the community champion or ridicule your actions? If you look the other way and avoid a lot of paperwork and hassle, will the community be disappointed or thankful?

Rebecca Kanable, "Turning off the Tap: Targeting Adults Who Violate MLDA Laws Stops the Flow of Alcohol to Youth and Prevents Other Problems," *Law Enforcement Technology*, vol. 32, issue 9, September 2005, pp. 80-88. Copyright 2005 Cygnus Business Media. All rights reserved. Reproduced by permission.

Underage drinking often seems to be a rite of passage. Eighty-three percent of adults who drink had their first drink of alcohol before age 21, according to the National Center on Addiction and Substance Abuse report on underage drinking released in February 2002.

Tolerance of Underage Drinking

James Fell, director of Traffic Safety and Enforcement Programs at the Pacific Institute for Research and Evaluation (PIRE) in Calverton, Maryland, compares today's overall attitude toward underage drinking in the United States to the attitude people had toward drunk driving in the 1960s and 1970s—it's tolerated. Not by everyone, he says, but a lot of people don't think underage drinking is a big deal.

Maybe if it's just one beer and no one gets in a car to drive home, underage drinking really isn't that much of a problem. Besides, aren't there more important things law enforcement officers should be doing than tracking down kids soaking up a few suds?

Responding to that devil's advocate thinking. Fell says "no," not in the sense that underage drinking is a huge public health problem that leads to youth endangering others and themselves. Underage drinking can lead to traffic deaths, suicides, homicides, unintentional injuries, assaults, rapes, alcohol dependence, vandalism and property damage—in addition to alcohol poisoning.

The effects of youth drinking alcohol can include long-term damage. Current research by the National Institutes of Health Institute of Mental Health and UCLA's Laboratory of Neuro Imaging shows the brain is not fully developed until about age 25. Early and excessive drinking at an early age can cause irreversible brain damage. Drinking before age 15 has been shown to cause problems in the future (from addiction, to drunk driving and assaults).

With underage drinking, one crime often leads to another.

"If you look at most communities, underage drinking is probably causing more problems than murders, robberies, burglaries, you name it," Fell says, noting exceptions might be found in communities that have a bigger problem with illegal drugs.

In the prevention of underage drinking and related problems, law enforcement plays a key role. A movement exists to re-target law enforcement efforts toward adults that illegally sell or provide alcohol to kids, says Traci Toomey, director of the Alcohol Epidemiology Program within the School of Public Health at the University of Minnesota in Minneapolis. "It is unlikely we have enough resources to create a deterrent effect by targeting underage drinkers," she says. "It is more likely we have enough resources to deter adults violating the minimum legal drinking age (MLDA) laws."

Attitudes

Alcohol is a drug, the No. 1 drug of choice among children and adolescents, reminds Fell, who serves on the National Board of Directors for Mothers Against Drunk Driving (MADD). If a community, and subsequently, the community's law enforcement officers don't see underage drinking as a big deal, he says the first step to underage drinking prevention needs to be an attitude change.

The National Academy of Sciences Institute of Medicine's 2003 "Underage Drinking: A Collective Responsibility" says: "There are signs that public attention to underage drinking is increasing and the public recognizes the need to address the problem more aggressively than has thus far occurred." . . .

Enforcement of Drinking Laws

The $61.9 billion-per-year (estimated cost of underage drinking) question is what can be done to stop youth from drinking alcohol.

The most effective tactic has been raising the minimum legal drinking age to 21. Because of this law, an estimated 900 to 1,000 lives per year in youth traffic deaths alone are saved, according to the National Highway Traffic Safety Administration.

Percentage of adults who think alcohol policies should focus more on people who provide alcohol to teenagers and less on teenagers who drink

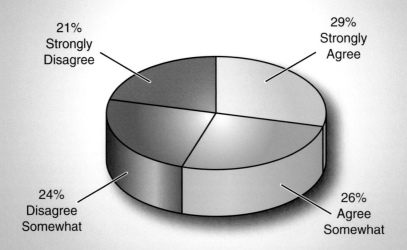

21%
Strongly
Disagree

29%
Strongly
Agree

24%
Disagree
Somewhat

26%
Agree
Somewhat

Taken from: Alcohol Epidemiology Program, University of Minnesota, "Youth Access to Alcohol Survey," December, 2002.

"Can you imagine how many lives would be saved if we enforced the law?" asks Fell, who worked at the NHTSA [National Highway Traffic and Safety Administration], as chief of research and evaluation for Traffic Safety Programs and manager of the Fatality Analysis Reporting System (FARS).

People think that the 21 drinking age law is the same in every state. The components of the drinking age law actually vary from state to state. There are 17 different components. The highest number of components a state has without loopholes and exceptions is 14, the least is three. Examples of components include: it's illegal for anyone under 21 to consume alcohol, it's illegal to use a fake ID, it's illegal for an adult to furnish alcohol to youth, it's illegal for an alcohol vendor to sell alcohol to youth, and it's illegal for any driver under age 21 to drive with any alcohol in their blood system (zero tolerance). Fell is working on a study looking at what components states have, how well they're enforced and whether enforcement reduces alcohol-related fatalities.

Joel Grube, director of the Prevention Research Center in Berkeley, California, says, "In a lot of ways enforcement is where the rubber hits the road. Law enforcement officers have a very important role to play in making sure the law is enforced because it is an effective prevention strategy."

A study by Grube, who holds a doctorate in social psychology, and Clyde Dent and Anthony Biglan of the Oregon Research Institute in Eugene, provides scientific evidence that underage drinking may be reduced by increasing enforcement of the minimum-age purchase laws and reducing the number of outlets that sell alcohol to kids. They found that underage drinking prevalence was lower in communities where young people perceived greater enforcement of underage drinking laws and where alcohol was more difficult to obtain. Their findings were published in "Community level alcohol availability and enforcement of possession laws as predictors of youth drinking," in the December 2004 *Preventative Medicine*.

Compliance Checks

One way to strongly deter sales to minors is police checks of establishments that sell alcohol. Research by Alexander Wagenaar at the University of Florida, and Toomey and Darin Erickson at the University of Minnesota found police checks are even more effective when they are repeated as often as every three months. During the compliance checks, an underage buyer attempts to buy alcohol without showing identification and violators are cited. Researchers found these checks work far better than programs that train bar and restaurant staff to identify and refuse service to minors.

"We found that enforcement has significant effects, but just like enforcement against any offense, you can't just do it once and think it solves everything," says Wagenaar, a professor of epidemiology and health policy research at the University of Florida's College of Medicine. "We have to create an ongoing perception on the part of the managers and owners of these establishments that they have a decent chance of getting caught if they sell to teenagers."

Law enforcement checks of liquor stores and other establishments selling alcohol for off-premise consumption produced an immediate 17-percent decrease in the subsequent likelihood of their selling to minors, researchers say. That reduction dissipated over time, from 11 percent two weeks after a check to 3 percent after two months. Most of the residual effect disappeared after three months.

Checks of bars and other on-premise establishments yielded even better results, with a 17-percent decrease immediately afterward diminishing to 14 percent at two weeks and 11 percent at two months.

Another finding of the research is compliance checks need to be checking all establishments regularly for preventative purposes.

Where kids get alcohol varies by age group, says Toomey. As kids get older, they might be more likely to try to sneak into bars, she says. While kids might have fake IDs, she says the purpose of compliance checks is to make sure establishments are doing the minimum of asking for IDs and checking them.

The study was carried out during a national downward trend in the tendency of alcohol establishments to sell to underage youth. In the early 1990s, the rate was 50 to 80 percent, Wagenaar says. In the research conducted by Wagenaar, Toomey and Erickson, the rate was roughly 20 percent.

"Communities have stepped up enforcement," he says. "There is much more carding going on now than in the '80s and '90s. There has been substantial progress, but most communities still pay way too little attention to enforcing the law against sales of alcohol to minors."

Shoulder Tap Campaigns

In addition to cutting off illegal sales, illegal provision must be cut off, especially since it is a more common means of youth obtaining alcohol, says Toomey, who holds a Ph.D. in epidemiology and is an associate professor.

In the Oregon study, 70 percent of youth got their alcohol from friends, parents or other social sources, while 30 percent got their alcohol from convenience stores, supermarkets or other commercial sources.

Although there is research supporting the effectiveness of compliance checks to cut off illegal sales, Toomey says there are only recommendations for what works to cut off illegal provision.

Shoulder tap campaigns have been effective in some communities. They are similar to compliance checks, but law enforcement has an underage person under their supervision approach an adult. If the adult agrees to purchase alcohol, it's an illegal act and the adult could be fined or arrested provided there are no concerns of entrapment. Or, a warning could be given saying if this had not been an educational campaign, a specific fine or jail term could have been issued.

Keg Registration Laws

Twenty-four states have keg registration laws. (Utah prohibits keg sales.) Retailers put a unique identifier on each keg. When someone purchases the keg, that person's name, driver's license number and other identifying information is recorded with the ID number of the keg.

If officers go to a house or an open field where they find a party and underage people drinking, and people flee the scene or no one will admit to purchasing the keg, officers can use the keg ID number to find the buyer and charge this person with illegal provision.

Social providers are often difficult to find, Toomey says. Keg registration is one tool to help locate them.

Education for Parents and Minors

How do you make people think they're likely to get caught if they provide alcohol to someone under 21? One way, if someone is arrested, is to make sure there is publicity about the arrest so it can be used as an opportunity to educate other adults, she says.

An underage investigative aide for Kentucky state law enforcement leaves a Food Mart with alcohol she just purchased. The store clerk failed to check her ID.

"I don't think a lot of adults really know what the laws are," says Toomey. "I'm still surprised when people ask if the legal drinking age is 21 in all states."

Whenever possible, she says law enforcement should both enforce and educate. She adds that education needs to go beyond the school setting because education in the schools alone has not sustained reductions in underage alcohol use.

She says in one small community police officers went so far as to visit the home of every high school senior before prom and gradua-tion, and informed students and their parents of the consequences of violating the minimum legal drinking age law.

Other Solutions

Other law enforcement tactics found to be effective against underage drinking include false ID detection machines; zero tolerance enforcement (no alcohol for drivers under the age of 21); and sobriety checkpoints, especially checkpoints using passive alcohol sensors.

To bring all the stakeholders together, community coalitions can be formed. For example, Communities Mobilizing for Change on Alcohol (CMCA) is a community organizing effort developed and evaluated by the Alcohol Epidemiology Program at the University of Minnesota. CMCA is designed to change policies and practices of major community institutions in ways that reduce access to alcohol by teenagers. To learn more about this community organizing effort see www.epi.umn.edu/alcohol/cmca/index.shtm.

Minnesota, like other states, has seen change thanks to its coalition, says Toomey, who serves on the National Board of Directors for MADD. In recent years community concerns have led to changes in the form of keg registration, a social host or civil cause of action and funding for compliance checks, she says.

Each community must look at what best fits its needs. Effective enforcement and prevention strategies include enforcing minimum age purchase laws and this can be done in conjunction with:

- Compliance checks
- Shoulder tap campaigns
- Keg registration laws
- Education that goes beyond schools.

Fell concludes, "There are lots of things that we can do. We just have to get serious about addressing the problem of underage drinking."

FIVE

It Is Up to Parents to Stop Underage Drinking

Joseph A. Califano Jr.

> In the following article, Joseph A. Califano Jr. argues that parents must take primary responsibility for stopping underage drinking. He points to a recent study that shows the wide availability of illegal drugs and alcohol in schools and argues that criminal laws are not enough to deter teens from drinking and drug use. Califano claims parental pessimism is making the problem worse and that parents need to recognize that only they have the power to keep their teens from drinking and using drugs. Joseph A. Califano Jr., chairman and president of the National Center on Addiction and Substance Abuse at Columbia University, was secretary of health, education, and welfare from 1977 to 1979.

The 10th annual survey of 12- to 17-year-olds by the National Center on Addiction and Substance Abuse at Columbia University (CASA) has a loud and clear message: Parents, if you want to raise drug-free kids, you cannot outsource your responsibility to their schools or law enforcement.

The odds are that drugs will be used, kept or sold—or all of the above—at the school your daughter or son attends and that

Joseph A. Califano Jr., "Parent Power," *America*, vol. 193, issue 13, October 31, 2005, pp. 13-15. All rights reserved. Reproduced by permission of America Press.

laws prohibiting teen use of tobacco, alcohol, marijuana and other illegal drugs will have little or no impact on your child's decision to smoke, drink or use marijuana.

It's All in the Family

What will motivate your kids to stay drug free is their perception of how Mom and Dad will react to their smoking, drinking or drug use, their sense of the immorality of such use for someone their age, and whether they consider such use harmful to their health. It is not much of an overstatement to say that reducing the risk of teen substance use is all in the family. Engaged and nourishing parents have the best shot at giving their children the will and skills to say no.

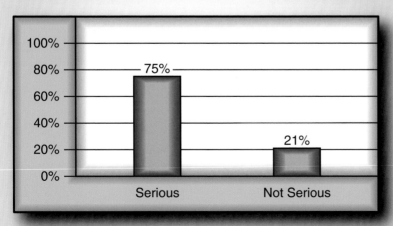

It Is Up to Parents to Stop Underage Drinking

2005 poll results: How serious is underage drinking in your community?

Taken from: ABC News Poll, July 15, 2005.

For any who doubt the frontline importance of the family in combating teen drug use and for parents who think they can outsource their responsibility, this year's CASA survey sends a grim message that a teen's world outside the family is infested with drugs.

The most disturbing finding is the extent to which our nation's schools are awash in alcohol, tobacco, and illegal and prescription drugs. Since 2002, the proportion of middle schoolers who say that drugs are used, kept or sold in their schools is up by a stunning 47 percent, and the proportion of high schoolers attending schools with drugs is up by 41 percent. This year, 10.6 million high schoolers, almost two-thirds, and 2.4 million middle schoolers, more than a quarter, are attending schools where drugs are used, kept or sold.

Sadly, many parents accept drug-infested schools as an inevitable part of their children's lives. Half of all parents surveyed report that drugs are used, kept or sold on the grounds of their teen's school, and a despairing 56 percent of these parents believe that the goal of making their child's school drug free is unrealistic. When asbestos is found in a school, most parents refuse to send their children there until it is removed; yet these same parents send their kids to drug-infected schools day after day. When parents feel as strongly about drugs in schools as they do about asbestos, they will give our teens a chance to be educated in a drug free environment.

The Price of Parental Pessimism

The price young people pay for parental pessimism and nonchalance is high. Teens who attend schools where drugs are used, kept or sold are three times likelier to try marijuana and get drunk in a typical month, compared with teens who attend drug-free schools. Students at high schools with drugs estimate that 44 percent of their schoolmates regularly use illegal drugs, compared with a 27 percent estimate by students at drug free schools.

This year's survey provides overwhelming additional evidence of the increasingly drug drenched world of American teens. In just one year, from 2004 to 2005, the percentage of 12- to 17-year-olds who know a friend or classmate who has abused prescription drugs jumped 86 percent; who has used the drug Ecstasy is up 28 percent; who has used illegal drugs, such as acid, cocaine or heroin, is up 20 percent.

Given the availability of substances throughout their lives—in their schools, among their friends—it is no wonder that teens continue to name drugs as their number one concern, as they have since CASA began conducting the survey in 1996. This year 29 percent of teens cite drugs as their top concern. (Remarkably, many parents don't understand this. Only 13 percent of those surveyed see drugs as their teens' biggest concern; almost 60 percent of parents consider social pressures their teens' biggest concern, a view only 22 percent of teens share.)

And little progress, if any, has been made in curtailing teens' ability to buy marijuana. Forty-two percent of 12- to 17-year-olds (11 million) can buy marijuana within a day; 21 percent (5.5 million) can buy it within an hour. This situation has remained unchanged over the past three years.

The abysmal failures of our schools to achieve and maintain a drug free status and of our government to reduce the availability of marijuana should by themselves be enough to alert parents to the critical significance of their role. But the clincher comes out of the mouths of teens themselves, who make it clear that morality and parental attitude trump illegality as deterrents to their smoking, drinking and drug use:

- Teens who believe smoking cigarettes or drinking alcohol by someone their age is "not morally wrong" are seven times likelier to smoke or drink than those who believe teen smoking is "seriously morally wrong."
- Teens whose parents would be "a little upset or not upset" if they smoked or drank are much likelier to smoke or drink than those whose parents would be "extremely upset."
- Teens who believe using marijuana is "not morally wrong" are 19 times likelier to use marijuana than teens who believe it is "seriously morally wrong."

- Teens who say their parents would be "a little upset" or "not upset at all" if they used marijuana are six times likelier to try marijuana than those whose parents would be "extremely upset."

Morality Comes from Parents

At the same time, most teens say legal restrictions have no impact on their decision to smoke cigarettes (58 percent) or drink alcohol (54 percent). Nearly half of teens say illegality plays no role in their decision to use marijuana, LSD, cocaine or heroin.

The point is not that criminal laws are irrelevant; they serve an important purpose to protect society and as a formal consensus of society's judgment about seriously harmful conduct. The point is that a child's sense of morality, which most 12- to 17-year-olds acquire from parents, and a clear appreciation of parental disapproval are far more powerful incentives to stay drug free.

Parents also have an important responsibility to monitor their children's conduct and know their children's friends. Forty-three percent of 12- to 17-year-olds see three or more R-rated movies in a typical month. These teens are seven times likelier to smoke cigarettes, six times likelier to try marijuana and five times likelier to drink alcohol than those who do not watch R-rated movies. Teens who report that half or more of their friends are sexually active are at nearly six times the risk for substance abuse as those teens with no sexually active friends. Similarly, teens who report that most of their friends drink or use marijuana are at much higher risk of substance abuse.

Parents Have the Power

The good news is that strong, positive family relationships are a powerful deterrent to teen smoking, drinking and drug use. Teens who would go to either or both their parents with a serious problem are at half the risk of teens who would seek out another adult. The substance-abuse risk for teens living in households with frequent family dinners, low levels of tension and stress among

Karolyn Nunnallee, National President of Mothers Against Drunk Driving (MADD) speaks at a Youth Leadership Power Camp. She is calling for changes to an Abercrombie & Fitch back-to-school catalog that contains drink recipes.

family members, parents who are proud of their teen and a parent in whom the teen can confide is half that of the average teen.

Frequent family dinners are a simple yet powerful way to influence teen behavior. Compared to teens who have at least five family dinners a week, those who have family dinner less often than three times a week are much likelier to smoke, drink and use marijuana. Only 13 percent of teens who have frequent family dinners have tried marijuana, compared with 35 percent of teens who have dinner with their parents no more than twice a week.

Teens who attend weekly religious services—or who say that religion is an important part of their lives—are at half the risk of smoking, drinking or using drugs as those who do not attend such services. And it is unlikely in this nation that 12- to 17-year-olds go to church each week without their parents.

Parent power is the greatest weapon we have to curb substance abuse. When mothers and fathers realize how much power they have—and use it sensitively—we will turn back this scourge that has destroyed so many children and brought so much grief to so many families and friends.

This nation's drug problem is all about kids. CASA's research has consistently shown that a child who gets through age 21 without smoking, abusing alcohol or using drugs is virtually certain never to do so. The CASA survey and 12 years of my life devoted to understanding this problem have led me to this bottom line: America's drug problem is not going to be solved in courtrooms, legislative hearing rooms or schoolrooms—or by judges, politicians or teachers. It will be solved in living rooms and dining rooms and across kitchen tables—and by parents and families.

SIX

It Is Not Possible to Stop Underage Drinking if the Drinking Age Is Twenty-One

William F. Buckley Jr.

> In the following article, William F. Buckley Jr. argues the law that sets the minimum drinking age at twenty-one is a bad law. He recounts an incident that was sensationalized in the media, where Jenna and Barbara Bush (daughters of President George W. Bush) were seen drinking, and they were both under the legal drinking age. Buckley notes that while alcohol can have harmful effects, enforcing the law is not possible. William F. Buckley Jr. is an author and commentator who founded the political magazine *National Review* in 1955.

We took one of those oaths not to write about the Bush ladies [Jenna and Barbara Bush, daughters of President George W. Bush; the media usually exercises restraint in reporting about the children of sitting presidents, particularly if the children are minors], but one aspect of their drinking affair is underplayed, which is the sheer idiocy of the law.

William F. Buckley Jr., "Jenna and Barbara, Honorary J.D.'s," *National Review*, vol. 53, issue 13, July 9, 2001, p. 54. Copyright © 2001 by National Review, Inc., 215 Lexington Avenue, New York, NY 10016. Reproduced by permission.

*Percentage who agree that punishments
for teenage drinking shouldn't be too severe*

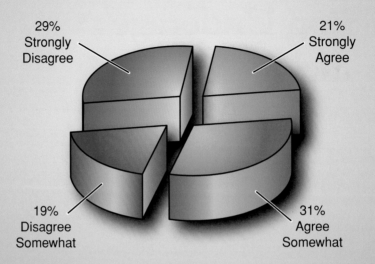

29%
Strongly
Disagree

21%
Strongly
Agree

19%
Disagree
Somewhat

31%
Agree
Somewhat

Taken from: Alcohol Epidemiology Program, University of Minnesota,
"Youth Access to Alcohol Survey," December 2002.

The Drinking Age

We all know that up until the counter-Woodstock anti-alcohol putsch of a generation ago, drinking was permitted in most states at age 18. Simultaneously, our lawmakers resolved a) to forbid drinking until age 21, and b) to permit voting at age 18.

Begin by acknowledging that alcoholism is the worst of our national curses. About 20 percent of Americans who drink, drink too much, and about 5 percent become alcoholics. They destroy family life, run over people while driving automobiles, aim pistols at their wives' lovers or at their wives, and commit suicide, sometimes belatedly. But those projections are not airtight, so that the most that can be said is that it pays to postpone alcoholic intake until a little supplementary seniority is there to contribute a bet-

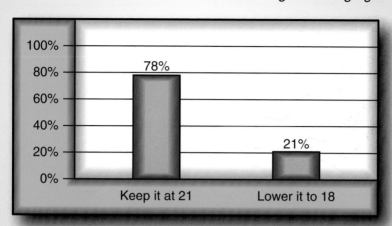

Is Lowering the Drinking Age the Solution?

How Americans feel about the minimum legal drinking age

- 78% — Keep it at 21
- 21% — Lower it to 18

Taken from: ABC News Poll, July 15, 2005.

ter perspective than you have at the earlier age. Certainly the perspective of Jenna and Barbara was off. To have slipped a drink when, it turns out, AP, Larry King, MGM, 60 *Minutes*, and Jim Lehrer were all staring at them from the corner of the restaurant shows an immature perspective.

But attempts to legislate on the basis of a prudent projection of the incidence of alcoholism are themselves misplaced acts of legislative/moral energy, because to choose one is glaringly to ignore that which you did not choose, which is, of course, tobacco. The statistics here are very firm. If you don't smoke until age 21, the chances are 90 percent that you will not smoke ever. And nicotine addiction, though it doesn't cause mayhem, does cause frequent and painful death.

The Problem of Enforcement

Now the argument against enforcing the rule against teenage smoking is that it is quite simply impossible. Who is so brave and so dumb as to stand up in front of a battery of policemen instruct-

College students enjoy a few beers at a pub in Cambridge, Massachusetts.

ing them to bring into court anyone with a cigarette in his mouth who can't prove that he was born before 1980? The move to repeal the constitutional amendment against drinking was fueled substantially by the national despair over its enforcement, and derivative gloom over the implications of wholesale resistance to the integrity of laws, let alone constitutionally specified laws.

Perhaps most of the time in Austin, Texas, the police do other things, and it is legitimately argued that the Bush ladies were simply dumb and provocative to ask for margaritas, let alone to produce other people's I.D. cards to disguise their ages. But whatever one might intone about the relative responsibilities of children of public figures, still the offense for which they were arraigned is better commentary on the misbehavior of the law, than of the two violators of it.

There are plenty of sanctions one can come up with against student drinkers who overdo it, and the reports a few months ago on binge drinking bring these to light. The Bush ladies have proved not much more than that modern life confirms that sexual equality means also the girls will be girls. Maybe when the two Bush sisters reach a venerable age they will be given honorary degrees by the University of Texas for having brought to focus, in the year 2001, the silliness of this particular blue law.

SEVEN

Lowering the Drinking Age Is Not the Solution

Robert Voas

> In the following article, Robert Voas argues that there is
> no benefit to lowering the drinking age, and he responds
> to several arguments in favor of lowering the age. After
> explaining that all of the arguments for lowering the
> drinking age fail, Voas concludes that the drinking age
> should remain twenty-one because lowering it would be
> very dangerous. Robert Voas is a senior research scientist
> at the Pacific Institute for Research and Evaluation.

After nearly four decades of exacting research on how to save
lives and reduce injuries by preventing drinking and driving,
there is a revanchist attempt afoot to roll back one of the most
successful laws in generations: the minimum legal drinking age
of 21.

This is extremely frustrating. While public health researchers
must produce painstaking evidence that's subjected to critical
scholarly review, lower-drinking-age advocates seem to dash off
remarks based on glib conjecture and self-selected facts.

It's startling that anybody—given the enormous bodies of
research and data—would consider lowering the drinking age.
And yet, legislation is currently pending in New Hampshire and
Wisconsin to lower the drinking age for military personnel and for

Robert Voas, "There's No Benefit to Lowering the Drinking Age," *The Christian Science Monitor,*
January 12, 2006, p. 9. Reproduced by permission of the author.

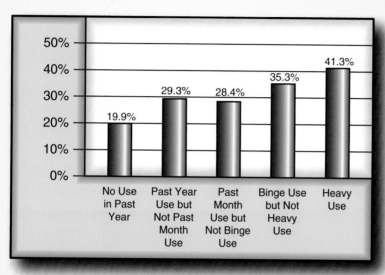

Drinking and Fighting

Percentages of youths aged 12 to 17 who took part in serious fighting at school or work in the past year, by level of alcohol use: 2003

- No Use in Past Year: 19.9%
- Past Year Use but Not Past Month Use: 29.3%
- Past Month Use but Not Binge Use: 28.4%
- Binge Use but Not Heavy Use: 35.3%
- Heavy Use: 41.3%

Taken from: National Survey on Drug Use and Health (NSDUH), 2005.

all residents in Vermont. Just as bad are the arguments from think-tank writers, various advocates, and even academics (including at least one former college president) that ignore or manipulate the real evidence and instead rely on slogans.

Responses to Arguments for Lowering the Drinking Age

I keep hearing the same refrains: "If you're old enough to go to war, you should be old enough to drink," or "the drinking-age law just increases the desire for the forbidden fruit," or "lower crash rates are due to tougher enforcement, not the 21 law," or "Europeans let their kids drink, so they learn how to be more responsible," or finally, "I did it when I was a kid, and I'm OK."

First, I'm not sure what going to war and being allowed to drink have in common. The military takes in youngsters particularly because they are not yet fully developed and can be molded into soldiers. The 21 law is predicated on the fact that drinking is more dangerous for youth because they're still developing mentally and physically, and they lack experience and are more likely to take risks. Ask platoon leaders and unit commanders, and they'll tell you that the last thing they want is young soldiers drinking.

Nineteen-year-old Lisa O'Connell was charged with drunk driving and motor vehicle homicide after she struck three pedestrians, one of whom died. Despite being underage, police say her blood alcohol level was 0.22 at the time of the accident.

As for the forbidden fruit argument, the opposite is true. Research shows that back when some states still had a minimum drinking age of 18, youths in those states who were under 21 drank more and continued to drink more as adults in their early 20s. In states where the drinking age was 21, teenagers drank less and continue to drink less through their early 20s.

And the minimum 21 law, by itself, has most certainly resulted in fewer accidents, because the decline occurred even when there was little enforcement and tougher penalties had not yet been enacted. According to the National Highway Traffic Safety Administration, the 21 law has saved 23,733 lives since states began raising drinking ages in 1975.

Do European countries really have fewer youth drinking problems? No, that's a myth. Compared to American youth, binge drinking rates among young people are higher in every European country except Turkey. Intoxication rates are higher in most countries; in Britain, Denmark, and Ireland they're more than twice the US level. Intoxication and binge drinking are directly linked to higher levels of alcohol-related problems, such as drinking and driving.

The Dangers of Lowering the Drinking Age

But, you drank when you were a kid, and you're OK. Thank goodness, because many kids aren't OK. An average of 11 American teens die each day from alcohol-related crashes. Underage drinking leads to increased teen pregnancy, violent crime, sexual assault, and huge costs to our communities. Among college students, it leads to 1,700 deaths, 500,000 injuries, 600,000 physical assaults, and 70,000 sexual assaults each year.

Recently, New Zealand lowered its drinking age, which gave researchers a good opportunity to study the impact. The result was predictable: The rate of alcohol-related crashes among young people rose significantly compared to older drivers.

I've been studying drinking and driving for nearly 40 years and have been involved in public health and behavioral health for 53 years. Believe me when I say that lowering the drinking age would be very dangerous; it would benefit no one except those who profit from alcohol sales.

If bars and liquor stores can freely provide alcohol to teenagers, parents will be out of the loop when it comes to their children's decisions about drinking. Age 21 laws are designed to keep such decisions within the family where they belong. Our society, particularly our children and grandchildren, will be immeasurably better off if we not only leave the minimum drinking age law as it is, but enforce it better, too.

TWELVE

American Youth Do Not Drink More than Their European Counterparts

Joel Grube

In the following report, Joel Grube addresses the common misperception that young people in America drink more often and have more alcohol-related problems than young people in European countries do. Using a 2003 survey that collected data from students in the United States and a 2003 survey that collected data from students in thirty-five European countries, Grube concludes that European youth drink more often and have higher intoxication rates than American youth. Joel Grube is social psychology director and a senior research scientist with the Pacific Institute for Research and Evaluation, an independent, nonprofit public health organization.

Among Americans there is a commonly held perception that American young people drink more frequently and experience more alcohol-related problems than do their European counterparts. This perception, in turn, is often utilized as argument for various changes in U.S. alcohol policies and prevention initiatives, including elimination of minimum drinking age laws

Pacific Institute for Research and Evaluation, Youth Drinking Rates and Problems: A Comparison of European Countries and the United States, 2005. Reproduced by permission.

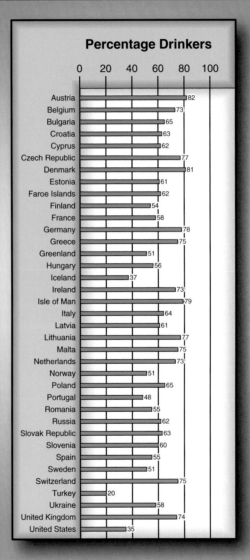

Prevalence of Drinking in the Past 30 Days: United States and Europe

Percentage Drinkers

Austria	82
Belgium	73
Bulgaria	65
Croatia	63
Cyprus	62
Czech Republic	77
Denmark	81
Estonia	61
Faroe Islands	62
Finland	54
France	58
Germany	78
Greece	75
Greenland	51
Hungary	56
Iceland	37
Ireland	73
Isle of Man	79
Italy	64
Latvia	61
Lithuania	77
Malta	75
Netherlands	73
Norway	51
Poland	65
Portugal	48
Romania	55
Russia	62
Slovak Republic	63
Slovenia	60
Spain	55
Sweden	51
Switzerland	75
Turkey	20
Ukraine	58
United Kingdom	74
United States	35

Taken from: 2003 ESPAD Survey and 2003
Monitoring the Future Survey

Figure 1

and development of programs that teach "responsible" drinking to young people.

Do European young people drink less and experience fewer problems than their American counterparts? Until recently data did not exist to easily answer this question, but new research demonstrates that this is not the case. In fact, in comparison with young people in the United States,

- A greater percentage of young people from nearly all European countries report drinking in the past 30 days;
- For a majority of these European countries, a greater percentage of young people report having five of more drinks in a row; and
- A great majority of the European countries have higher intoxication rates among young people than the United States and less than a quarter had lower rates or equivalent rates to the United States.

Based on this analysis, the comparison of drinking rates and alcohol-related problems among young people in the United States and in European countries does not provide support for elimination of U.S. minimum drinking age laws or for the implementation of programs to teach responsible drinking to young people.

Comparing European and U.S. Drinking Habits

Do young people from Europe drink more responsibly than do young people from the United States?
This question is important because it often is raised in the context of the stricter minimum drinking age laws in the United States. Although the implementation of the uniform minimum drinking age of 21 and the more recent enactment of zero tolerance laws have reduced drinking by young people and saved thousands of lives, these policies have come under attack as contributing to irresponsible styles of drinking. Commonly, European countries

are held up as examples of where more liberal drinking age laws and attitudes, in turn, may foster more responsible styles of drinking by young people. It often is asserted that alcohol is more integrated into European, especially southern European, culture and that young people there learn to drink at younger ages within the context of the family. As a result, it is further asserted that young Europeans learn to drink more responsibly than do young people from the United States.

A girl drinks a glass of wine at a bar in Prague, Czech Republic. The Pacific Institute for Research and Evaluation argues that youth drinking is a more common and more serious problem in Europe than in the United States.

This report addresses the question of whether young people in Europe actually drink more responsibly than those in the United States. Data for this paper come from the 2003 European School Survey Project on Alcohol and Other Drugs (ESPAD) and the 2003 United States Monitoring the Future Survey (MTF).

European School Survey Project on Alcohol and Other Drugs (ESPAD)

The ESPAD survey collected data in 2003 from 15- to 16-year-old students in 35 European countries. The data were obtained using anonymous self-administered in-school surveys. Sample sizes ranged from 555 (Greenland) to 5,110 (Germany). The samples were designed to be nationally representative in each case. Because not all questions were asked in all countries, the data reported here are based on somewhat fewer than 35 countries. A detailed report on the methods and findings from the ESPAD survey is available.

Monitoring the Future Survey (MTF)

The MTF survey is conducted annually among 8th, 10th, and 12th graders in the United States. The samples are designed to be nationally representative of students in those grade levels. The data reported here are for the 10th grade sample because it represents the same age group that was included in the ESPAD surveys. The 10th grade MTF survey comprises an anonymous self-administered questionnaire given in the school setting. The 2003 MTF survey included 18,500 10th graders. Detailed descriptions of the MTF methods and findings may be found on the Internet (http://monitoringthefuture.org/) or in a series of publications available from the National Institute on Drug Abuse.

Comparability

The questionnaire for the ESPAD survey was closely modeled after the MTF survey. Most of the questions from the two surveys map closely onto one another. One notable difference is in the heavy episodic or binge drinking question (i.e., "how many times have you had five or more drinks in a row?"). Specifically, the ESPAD

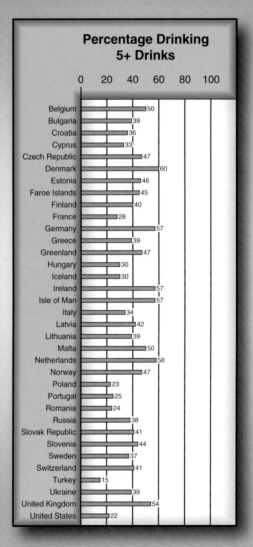

Prevalence of Heavy Drinking in the Past 30 Days: United States and Europe

Percentage Drinking 5+ Drinks

Country	Percentage
Belgium	50
Bulgaria	39
Croatia	36
Cyprus	33
Czech Republic	47
Denmark	60
Estonia	46
Faroe Islands	45
Finland	40
France	28
Germany	57
Greece	39
Greenland	47
Hungary	30
Iceland	30
Ireland	57
Isle of Man	57
Italy	34
Latvia	42
Lithuania	39
Malta	50
Netherlands	58
Norway	47
Poland	23
Portugal	25
Romania	24
Russia	38
Slovak Republic	41
Slovenia	44
Sweden	37
Switzerland	41
Turkey	15
Ukraine	39
United Kingdom	54
United States	22

Taken from: 2003 ESPAD Survey and 2003 Monitoring the Future Survey

Figure 2

survey asks this question in terms of the last 30 days, whereas the MTF survey asks about the previous 2 weeks.

Survey Results Show U.S. Youth Drink Less

Prevalence of Drinking in Past 30 Days

Figure 1 shows the percentage of young people in 35 European countries and the United States reporting that they had at least one drink of any alcoholic beverage during the past 30 days. These 30-day prevalence rates are often used as an indicator of the number of current or regular drinkers in a population. In the 2003 MTF survey, 35 percent of 10th graders reported that they had a drink in the past 30 days. It is clear from Figure 1 that the United States is a low consumption country by European standards. With the exception of Turkey (20%), every European country in the ESPAD survey had higher prevalence rates. In most cases, the rates of current drinking far exceeded those observed in the United States. Iceland (37%) and the United States had essentially equivalent prevalence rates on this measure.

Prevalence of Heavy Drinking (Having Five or More Drinks in a Row)

Although the data in Figure 1 show that fewer American adolescents are current drinkers than is the case for a vast majority of European countries, what is not clear is if the patterns of drinking are such that European adolescents are more at risk for problems. It may be, for example, that more of them drink, but do so moderately in a family context. Consuming five or more drinks in a row is one measure of heavy episodic or "binge" drinking that is frequently used. This style of drinking is known to be associated with increased risk for a number of problems including DUI, fighting, truancy, and involvement in criminal activities such as theft, burglary, and assault. The prevalence of binge drinking from the ESPAD and MTF surveys is shown in Figure 2. If the early socialization to drinking that is assumed to be typical of Europe is such that it fosters responsible drinking, then we would expect to

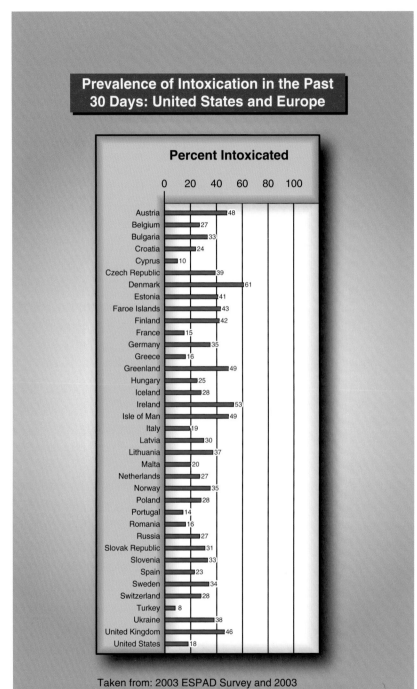

Figure 3

see much lower rates of binge drinking there than in the United States. Contrary to these expectations, U.S. adolescents show lower prevalence rates for drinking five or more drinks in a row than most European countries in the ESPAD survey. In many cases, the percentage of young people reporting drinking five or more drinks in a row is considerably higher than that for the United States. Only Turkey (15%) has a substantially lower rate than is seen for the United States (22%). It should be noted that the rates for the United States are lower than those for Italy (34%) or Greece (39%), countries that could be considered typically southern European. Data for Austria and Spain are missing.

Intoxication

Another measure of problematic drinking is intoxication. Unlike the measures of binge drinking, the items addressing intoxication were identical between the ESPAD and MTF surveys. Thus, direct comparisons can be made with certainty. As with binge drinking, intoxication is associated with a wide variety of personal and social problems. To the extent that the more liberal policies and attitudes toward drinking in Europe contribute to a more responsible drinking style among adolescents, one would expect to find lower rates of intoxication among young Europeans. Figure 3 displays the 30-day prevalence rates for self-reported intoxication for European and American adolescents. As with binge drinking, adolescents from the United States show a moderate rate of intoxication (18%) compared with their European peers. The United States is somewhat higher on this measure than some countries (e.g., Cyprus, France, Greece, Portugal, Romania, Turkey), substantially lower than others (e.g., Austria, Denmark, Finland, Greenland, Ireland, Isle of Man, United Kingdom), and essentially equivalent to still others (e.g., Italy, Malta). Only for Turkey and Cyprus are the prevalence rates substantially lower than for the United States. There is no evidence that the stricter laws and policies regarding drinking by young people in the United States are associated with higher rates of intoxication. Equally, there is no evidence that the more liberal policies and drinking socialization practices in Europe are associated with lower levels of intoxication.

Europeans Do Not Drink More Responsibly

Recent data from representative surveys provide no evidence that young Europeans drink more responsibly than their counterparts in the United States.

- A greater percentage of young people from nearly all European countries in the survey report drinking in the past 30 days.
- For a majority of these European countries, a greater percentage of young people report having five or more drinks in a row compared to U.S. 10th graders. Only for Turkey did a lower percentage of young people report this behavior.
- A great majority of the European countries in the survey had higher prevalence rates for self-reported intoxication than the United States, less than a quarter had lower rates, and less than a quarter had rates that were more or less the same as the United States.

NINE

Supervised Underage Drinking in the Home Should Be Allowed

Radley Balko

> In the following article, Radley Balko, policy analyst and author, explains how parents have started to throw parties and serve alcohol at home for their kids, so they can supervise and protect them. Some of these parents have been arrested for providing alcohol to minors. Balko argues that these parents ought to be commended instead of arrested for creating a safe environment for an activity the kids would engage in anyway. Balko is the author of the study, *Back Door to Prohibition: The New War on Social Drinking.*

Imagine for a moment that you're a parent with a teenage son. He doesn't drink, but you know his friends do. You're also not naive. You've read the government's statistics: 47 percent of high school students tell researchers they've had a drink of alcohol in the previous 30 days. Thirty percent have had at least five drinks in a row in the past month. Thirteen percent admitted to having driven in the previous month after drinking alcohol.

Radley Balko, "Zero Tolerence Makes Zero Sense," *The Washington Post*, August 9, 2005, p. A17. Reproduced by permission of the author.

Parents Throwing Parties

So, what do you do with regard to your son's social life? Many parents have decided to take a realist's approach. They're throwing parties for their kids and their friends. They serve alcohol at these parties, but they also collect car keys to make sure no one drives home until the next morning. Their logic makes sense: The kids are going to drink; it's better that they do it in a controlled, supervised environment.

Marcy Spiwak of Skokie, Illinois was charged with allowing her home to be used for underage drinking.

That's exactly what a Rhode Island couple did in 2004. When they learned that their son planned to celebrate the prom with a booze bash at a beach 40 miles away, William and Patricia Anderson instead threw a supervised party for him and his friends at their home. They served alcohol, but William Anderson stationed himself at the party's entrance and collected keys from every teen who showed. No one who came to the party could leave until the next morning.

For this the Andersons found themselves arrested and charged with supplying alcohol to minors. The case ignited a fiery debate that eventually spilled onto the front page of the *Wall Street Journal*. The local chapter of Mothers Against Drunk Driving oddly decided to make an example of William Anderson, a man who probably did more to keep drunk teens off the road that night than most Providence-area parents.

In fact, the Andersons were lucky. A couple in Virginia was recently sentenced to 27 months in jail for throwing a supervised party for their son's 16th birthday, at which beer was made available. That was reduced on appeal from the eight-year sentenced imposed by the trial judge. The local MADD president said she was "pleasantly surprised" at the original eight-year verdict, and "applauded" the judge's efforts.

Parents Should Not Be Punished

In the Washington area, several civic groups, public health organizations and government agencies have teamed up for a campaign called Party Safe 2005. You may have heard the ads on local radio stations in prom season, warning parents that law enforcement would be taking a zero-tolerance approach to underage drinking. The commercials explicitly said that even supervised parties—such as those where parents collect the keys of partygoers—wouldn't be spared. Parents would risk jail time and a fine of $1,000 per underage drinker.

Not only do such uncompromising approaches do little to make our roads safer, they often make them worse. The data don't lie. High school kids drink, particularly during prom season. We might

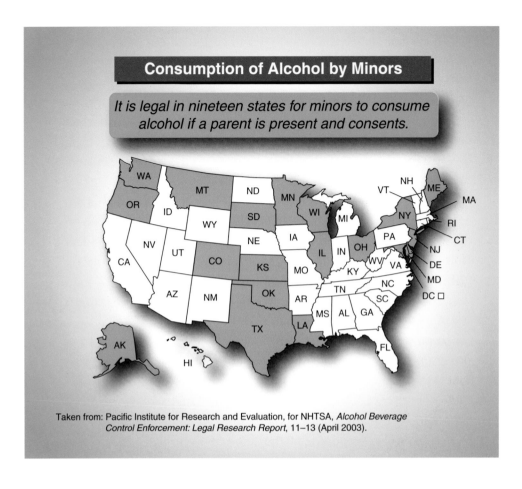

Consumption of Alcohol by Minors

It is legal in nineteen states for minors to consume alcohol if a parent is present and consents.

Taken from: Pacific Institute for Research and Evaluation, for NHTSA, *Alcohol Beverage Control Enforcement: Legal Research Report*, 11–13 (April 2003).

not be comfortable with that, but it's going to happen. It always has. The question, then, is do we want them drinking in their cars, in parking lots, in vacant lots and in rented motel rooms? Or do we want them drinking at parties with adult supervision, where they're denied access to the roads once they enter?

The Virginia case mentioned above is troubling for another reason: The cops raided that home without a search warrant. This is becoming more and more common in jurisdictions with particularly militant approaches to underage drinking. A prosecutor in Wisconsin popularized the practice in the late 1990s when he authorized deputies to enter private residences without warrants, "by force, if necessary," when there was the slightest suspicion of underage drinking. For such "innovative" approaches, Paul

Bucher won plaudits from Mothers Against Drunk Driving, which awarded him a place in the "Prosecutors as Partners" honor roll on the MADD Web site.

The *Post* reported a while back on a party in Bethesda in which there was no underage drinking at all. Police approached the parents at a backyard graduation party and asked if they could administer breath tests to underage guests. The mother refused. So the cops cordoned off the block and administered breath tests to each kid as he or she left the party. Not a single underage guest had been drinking. The police then began writing traffic tickets for all of the cars around the house hosting the party. The mother told the *Post*, "It almost seemed like they were angry that they didn't find anything."

Surely there are more pressing concerns for the Washington area criminal justice system to address than parents who throw supervised parties for high school kids. These parents are at least involved enough in their kids' lives to know that underage drinking goes on and to take steps to prevent that reality from becoming harmful. We ought to be encouraging that kind of thing, not arresting people for it.

TEN

Supervised Underage Drinking in the Home Should Not Be Allowed

Michael Shapiro

> In the following article, Michael Shapiro argues against proposed laws that would allow underage drinking in the home. Shapiro claims that allowing drinking in the home would contribute to the problem of underage drinking, and he believes that adults who allow underage drinking in their homes should face legal punishment. He describes underage drinking as a serious problem that needs to be addressed by greater parental involvement and personal responsibility. Michael Shapiro is an attorney, who resides in New Providence, New Jersey, and he is editor of the *Alternative Press*.

Recently, the Mountainside, New Jersey Police Department dropped its plan to file charges against fifty-six teenagers found drinking alcoholic beverages at a party in a private home. Why? According to a report in the *Star-Ledger*, both the Union County Prosecutor's Office, as well as the Office of the State Attorney General, have concluded that state law only prohibits the consumption or possession of alcohol by anyone underage as long as it takes place, "in any school, public conveyance, public place, or place of public assembly, or motor vehicle." However, the law does not cover underage people who engage in such activity

Michael Shapiro, "It's Time to Seriously Address Underage Drinking," *www.shaptalk.com*, April 29, 2007. Reproduced by permission.

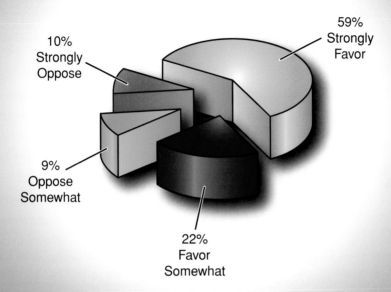

Poll on Social Host Liability Laws (laws that make it easier to sue an adult if harm results from giving alcohol to a minor)

59%
Strongly
Favor

10%
Strongly
Oppose

9%
Oppose
Somewhat

22%
Favor
Somewhat

Taken from: Alcohol Epidemiology Program, University of Minnesota, "Youth Access to Alcohol Survey," December 2002.

in the privacy of a home. Meanwhile, the 51-year old father of the teen who apparently hosted the party still faces charges. The incident raises some interesting questions.

No Privacy for Underage Drinkers

First, should the state law be amended to include a prohibition on the underage possession or consumption of alcohol in a private home? On the surface, the answer is yes. Underage drinking is a scourge that is overtaking our communities resulting in increased crime, and of course, damage to the health and well-being of underage drinkers themselves. However, there is a small but growing movement afoot that argues that it is better for the underage drinking to be taking place in a private home, especially under parental supervision, than elsewhere. Therefore, this movement argues, by amending the law, the private home becomes off-limits, leading teens to drink in far more undesirable locations. While this position accepts the idea that underage drinking is a problem, it helps contribute to it rather than seeking to eradicate it. Therefore, the state law should be amended to make underage drinking in private homes illegal.

Second, should parents who are at home during underage drinking parties face fines and jail time? Again, the answer is yes. Parents who condone, or even encourage, underage drinking in their own homes should face stiff fines and penalties including jail time. However, is it better to have parents home if underage

A mock legislative panel hears testimony from high school students in Hartford, Connecticut. The students are calling for tougher laws that crack down on adults who host private parties where youth can drink alcohol.

drinking will occur anyway? An adult that allows underage drinking parties in his home should be punished to the fullest extent of the law. Why? It is one thing for a parent to allow his own child to drink in his home. It is another matter to allow other children to drink, thereby exposing them to the very real dangers that underage drinking pose.

Underage Drinking Is a Big Problem

Third, is underage drinking a real problem facing our communities or is it a minor issue in only some towns? Underage drinking is a pandemic in New Jersey's municipalities and beyond. Residents who argue otherwise may fool themselves, but statistics and anecdotal evidence suggest otherwise. It is clear that alcohol counseling in our public schools has largely failed, leading our youth to drink hard and often.

Fourth, what can we do to stem the tide of underage drinking in our communities? Greater parental involvement in our children's lives is needed and greater personal responsibility on the part of both children and their parents must be taken. Adults need to teach their children the dangers of underage drinking and enforce a strict zero-tolerance policy towards it. In addition, our municipalities should be exploring opportunities to keep children away from alcohol, including night-time sports activities, a township community center where youth can play games, practice crafts, have pizza parties, and engage in other healthy activities. Most importantly, our elected officials must stop denying there is a problem and encouraging police departments under their jurisdiction to turn a blind eye towards it. They need to provide training and support to our teachers so that they can recognize the signs of alcoholism in our youth and report it accordingly. They also have to provide the resources to our municipalities to create healthy alternatives for our children.

The issue of underage drinking is one that is conveniently swept under the rug in our towns. Elected officials do not want to touch it, parents look the other way, and as a result, our children are suffering. How many drunk driving fatalities will it take before we see change? How many more children must suffer liver damage and many other ailments before underage drinking is appropriately addressed?

The sad truth is that until it is your underage son or your daughter who is killed by binge drinking or is otherwise directly and negatively impacted by underage drinking, you will either continue to pretend underage drinking does not exist or that it exists and there is nothing that can be done about it. Both positions are not only foolhardy but also incredibly dangerous, both for our children and our communities.

What You Should Know About Underage Drinking

Facts About Alcohol

- Humans have consumed alcoholic beverages for thousands of years. Evidence suggests humans consumed alcohol as early as 9,000 years ago in China and the Middle East.
- Alcoholic beverages contain ethanol. Ethanol is a very strong smelling, colorless, volatile liquid, formed by the fermentation of sugars.
- Alcoholic beverages are made from foods containing sugar or starch such as barley, rye, rice, pears, grapes, ginger, potatoes, milk, beets, honey, and bananas.
- A twelve-ounce beer has about as much alcohol as a five-ounce glass of wine or a 1.5-ounce shot of liquor.
- Some religions, such as Islam, the Church of Jesus Christ of Latter-day Saints, Sikhism, Seventh-Day Adventists, and Bahaism forbid, discourage, or restrict alcohol consumption.

Facts About the Dangers of Alcohol

- According to the National Institutes of Health, alcohol was involved in 36 percent of traffic deaths among sixteen- to twenty-year-olds in 2004.
- The U.S. Department of Transportation estimates that raising the drinking age to twenty-one has resulted in a thousand fewer traffic deaths each year.

- Consuming large quantities of alcohol within a short period of time can lead to death due to respiratory depression.
- Women who drink alcohol during pregnancy may give birth to infants with fetal alcohol syndrome.
- Many medicines—prescription and over-the-counter—can be dangerous when mixed with alcohol.

Facts About State Drinking Age Laws
- There are hundreds of "dry" counties in the United States, where the sale of alcoholic beverages is forbidden. States with dry counties include Alabama, Texas, Kentucky, and Mississippi.
- The District of Columbia has decriminalized underage drinking, making consumption of alcohol by those under age twenty-one a civil rather than a criminal offense. Offenders are no longer arrested.
- In Nebraska state law prohibits bars from selling beer unless they are simultaneously brewing a kettle of soup.
- In Wisconsin an adult under the age of twenty-one whose spouse is twenty-one or older can legally drink with his or her spouse.
- In many states, only beverages with lower alcohol content by volume (such as beer and wine) can be sold at supermarkets and convenience stores while hard liquor can only be purchased at state-run liquor stores.

Facts About Parents and Alcohol
- According to the 2003 National Academy of Sciences Report, two-thirds of teens who drink get alcohol from their parents or other adults.
- According to the 2004 Roper Youth Report, 75 percent of teenagers ages thirteen to seventeen say their parents are the main influence in their decisions about whether or not to drink alcohol.
- Recent polls by the American Medical Association reveal that 10 percent of parents think it is fine for teens to go to gradu-

ation parties with alcohol if a parent is present. Meanwhile, 20 percent of sixteen- to eighteen-year-olds report they have attended such a graduation party.

- According to a report from the Substance Abuse and Mental Health Services Administration, almost 5 million alcohol-dependent or alcohol-abusing parents have at least one child living at home with them.
- Children with an alcoholic parent are more likely to become alcoholics themselves.

What You Should Do About Underage Drinking

The subject of underage drinking raises many concerns. There are facts you need to be aware of before making any decisions. This includes being aware of the law and legal issues concerning underage drinking and knowing the facts about the effects of underage drinking. There are situations that you may face where you need to be prepared. You may face peer pressure to engage in underage drinking or you may have friends that have a problem with alcohol. You also need to decide where you stand on the issues and determine whether or not you want to become actively involved with these issues.

Know the Facts

While all states have laws against the purchase and public possession of alcohol for those under twenty-one, laws about private possession and consumption vary widely from state to state. Some states allow private consumption of alcohol in the home, if supplied by parents, but others do not. Similarly, some states provide exceptions for the possession of alcohol while engaged in legitimate employment. Research your own state's laws by visiting your state government's Web site or going to the library.

Alcohol affects the body and affects younger people differently than older people. Know the facts about alcohol and the effects it can have. There are many books, periodicals, and Web sites devoted to the topic, and there are several resources listed in the "For Further Reading" chapter of this book. Additionally, many organizations offer information on the effects of alcohol. Those listed in the "Organizations to Contact" chapter in this book are good places to start. Visit your local library for further information about other resources.

Personal Decisions

Deciding ahead of time how you will react if you are offered alcohol is one way to be prepared. Many of the organizations listed in the chapter "Organizations to Contact" have information and tools for young people who are faced with situations where alcohol is present. Talking to your parents and other adults about this issue is a good place to start.

You may be faced with a situation where others around you are drinking. Think about how you would react if you were asked to get in a car with a driver who had been drinking. Talk to your parents about how they would want you to react. Find out if there are local services available that you can use if you find yourself in this kind of situation. For example, many cities and college campuses have groups that provide free rides home to those who have been drinking.

Know what to do if you have a friend who needs help with a drinking problem. There are groups that offer resources to help diagnose and treat problems with alcohol. These groups can be easily found on the Internet.

Activism

There are many contentious issues surrounding underage drinking. The minimum age is one issue that is continually debated. You may decide that you want to get involved in this issue, either by working to lower the drinking age or by working to keep the age at twenty-one. Education is another issue you may want to get involved in. Strategies for promoting responsible drinking vary. For example, some groups promote abstinence, while others promote drinking in moderation. Decide what you think and then help educate your peers.

In order to determine if you would like to get more involved, visit the Web sites of some of the organizations listed in "Organizations to Contact" or those of other organizations you find through your own research. Be sure to review what an organization's stated goal or mission is and make sure that you understand where the organization stands on the issues important to you. If you find an organization that matches your interests, contact it and ask how you can get involved.

Americans for a Society Free from Age Restrictions (ASFAR)
PO Box 11358, Chicago, IL 60611
Web site: www.asfar.org

ASFAR is an organization dedicated to protecting and advancing the legal civil rights of youth. The organization fights the voting age, curfew laws, and other laws that limit the freedom of young people. ASFAR publishes the quarterly magazine *Youth Truth*.

The Center on Alcohol Marketing and Youth (CAMY)
Health Policy Institute, Georgetown University, Box 571444
3300 Whitehaven Street NW, Suite 5000, Washington, DC 20057
(202) 687-1019
e-mail: info@camy.org
Web site: http://camy.org

CAMY monitors the marketing practices of the alcohol industry. Its goal is to reduce underage alcohol consumption by using the public health strategies of limiting the access to and the appeal of alcohol to underage persons. Its Web site offers fact sheets, research reports, and press releases.

Center for Science in the Public Interests—Alcohol Policies Project
1875 Connecticut Avenue NW, #300, Washington, DC 20009
(202) 332-9110 ext. 385
e-mail: alcproject@cspinet.org
Web site: www.cspinet.org

The Alcohol Policies Project works to focus public policy maker attention on reforms to reduce the health and social consequences of drinking. Its Web site offers information about current projects, news releases, action alerts, and a wide variety of publications, including *Preventing Youth Access to Alcohol from Commercial Sources.*

Choose Responsibility
PO Box 507, Middlebury, VT 05753
(802) 398-2024
e-mail: info@chooseresponsibility.org
Web site: www.chooseresponsibility.org

Choose Responsibility works to engage young people, their parents, and public officials in serious deliberation about the role of alcohol in American culture. The organization advocates a multifaceted approach that combines education, certification, and provisional licensing for eighteen- to twenty-year-old high school graduates who choose to consume alcohol. Its Web site offers facts about underage drinking and a model alcohol education curriculum.

Leadership to Keep Children Alcohol Free
c/o The CDM Group, Inc.
7500 Old Georgetown Road, Suite 900, Bethesda, MD 20814
(301) 654-6740
e-mail: leadership@alcoholfreechildren.org
Web site: www.alcoholfreechildren.org

Leadership to Keep Children Alcohol Free strives to prevent early use of alcohol by children by educating the public about early alcohol use and focusing the attention of state and national policy makers on the seriousness of the early onset of alcohol use. Its Web site offers statistics, research, prevention resources, and publications, including *How Does Alcohol Affect the World of a Child?*

Mothers Against Drunk Driving (MADD)
511 East John Carpenter Freeway, Suite 700, Irving, TX 75062
(800) 438-6233
Web site: www.madd.org

MADD's mission is to stop drunk driving, support the victims of this violent crime, and prevent underage drinking. Its Web site offers position papers and publications, including *Underage Drinking: You're Stronger than You Think*. MADD publishes the biannual magazine *Driven*.

National Center on Addiction and Substance Abuse (CASA) at Columbia University
633 Third Avenue, Nineteenth Floor, New York, NY 10017
(212) 841-5200
Web site: www.casacolumbia.org

CASA aims to inform Americans of the economic and social costs of substance abuse and its impact on their lives, while also removing the stigma of substance abuse and replacing shame and despair with hope. CASA publishes numerous reports and books, including *Women Under the Influence*.

National Council on Alcoholism and Drug Dependence (NCADD)
244 East 58th Street, Fourth Floor, New York, NY 10022
(212) 269-7797
e-mail: national@ncadd.org
Web site: www.ncadd.org

The NCADD works to fight the stigma and the disease of alcoholism and other drug addictions. It publishes numerous pamphlets including *What Are the Signs of Alcoholism?* and *Drinking Too Much Too Fast Can Kill You*. In addition, it publishes the *Washington Report*, a monthly Washington, D.C.–based public policy newsletter, and *NCADD Amethyst*, a quarterly informational newsletter covering major issues in the field.

National Institute on Alcohol Abuse and Alcoholism (NIAAA)
5635 Fishers Lane, MSC 9304, Bethesda, MD 20892
(301) 443-3860
Web site: www.niaaa.nih.gov

The NIAAA aims to reduce alcohol-related problems by conducting research and disseminating research findings to health-care providers, researchers, policy makers, and the public. It publishes the quarterly bulletin *Alcohol Alert* for researchers and health professionals. For the general public, it publishes pamphlets, brochures, fact sheets, and the newsletter *Frontlines.*

National Youth Rights Association (NYRA)
1133 Nineteenth Street NW, Ninth Floor, Washington, DC 20036
(202) 833-1200 ext. 5714
Web site: www.youthrights.org

NYRA works to defend the civil and human rights of young people in the United States. It is a youth-led organization that supports lowering the drinking age, lowering the voting age, repealing government curfews, protecting student rights, and fighting age discrimination. Its Web site offers position papers, research, news, and discussion forums.

Students Against Destructive Decisions (SADD)
255 Main Street, Marlborough, MA 01752
(877) 723-3462
e-mail: info@sadd.org
Web site: www.sadd.org

SADD provides students with prevention and intervention tools to deal with the issues of underage drinking, other drug use, impaired driving, and other decisions. Its Web site offers news and links to articles published by the organization elsewhere. SADD publishes the newsletter *Decisions.*

Substance Abuse and Mental Health Services Administration (SAMHSA)
5600 Fishers Lane, Rockville, MD 20857
(301) 443-8956
Web site: www.samhsa.gov

SAMHSA works to build resilience and facilitate recovery for people with or at risk for mental or substance use disorders. Among its programs are "Too Smart to Start," an underage alcohol use prevention initiative, and "Family Guide," a public education program developed to support the efforts of parents to prevent the use of alcohol, tobacco, and illegal drugs among seven- to eighteen-year-olds. Its Web site includes links to its programs, each of which contains various publications, research, and advice.

Underage Drinking Enforcement Training Center (UDETC)
Pacific Institute for Research and Evaluation
11720 Beltsville Drive, Suite 900, Calverton, MD 20705
(877) 335-1287
e-mail: udetc@udetc.org
Web site: www.udetc.org

Established by the Office of Juvenile Justice and Delinquency Prevention, UDETC works to limit youth access to alcohol by providing a wide variety of science-based, practical, and effective training assistance services. The organization hosts electronic seminars and annual leadership conferences. It develops publications, such as the *Guide for Preventing and Dispersing Underage Drinking Parties*, to assist states and communities in their efforts to enforce underage drinking laws and prevent conditions that contribute to underage drinking.

Books

Institute of Medicine National Research Council of the National Academies, Richard J. Bonnie, and Mary Ellen O'Connell, eds., *Reducing Underage Drinking: A Collective Responsibility*. Washington, DC: National Academy Press, 2004.

Katherine Ketcham, *Teens Under the Influence: The Truth About Kids, Alcohol, and Other Drugs—How to Recognize the Problem and What to Do About It*. New York: Ballantine Books, 2003.

Cynthia Kuhn et al., *Buzzed: The Straight Facts About the Most Used and Abused Drugs from Alcohol to Ecstasy*. New York: Norton, 2003.

Marilyn McClellan, *The Big Deal About Alcohol: What Teens Need to Know About Drinking*. Berkeley Heights, NJ: Enslow, 2004.

Barrett Seaman, *Binge: Campus Life in an Age of Disconnection and Excess*. Indianapolis, IN: Wiley, 2006.

Joyce Brennfleck Shannon, ed., *Alcohol Information for Teens: Health Tips About Alcohol and Alcoholism*. Detroit, MI: Omnigraphics, 2004.

Chris Volkmann and Toren Volkmann, *From Binge to Blackout: A Mother and Son Struggle with Teen Drinking*. New York: NAL Trade, 2006.

Henry Wechsler and Bernice Wuethrich, *Dying to Drink: Confronting Binge Drinking on College Campuses*. Emmaus, PA: Rodale, 2003.

Periodicals

Burlington Free Press, "Lowering Drinking Age No Solution to Abuse," February 27, 2007.

George W. Dowdall, "The Functions and Dysfunctions of Youth Alcohol Use," *Nutrition Today*, January–February 2003.

Rutger C.M.E. Engels, "Beneficial Functions of Alcohol Use in Adolescents: Theory and Implications for Prevention," *Nutrition Today*, January–February 2003.

Brian S. Flynn et al., "Mass Media and Community Interventions to Reduce Alcohol Use by Early Adolescents," *Journal of Studies on Alcohol*, January 2006.

Kimberly L. Henry, Michael D. Slater, and Eugene R. Oetting, "Alcohol Use in Early Adolescence: The Effect of Changes in Risk Taking, Perceived Harm and Friends' Alcohol Use," *Journal of Studies on Alcohol*, March 2005.

Megan James, "Lower Drinking Age," *Addison Independent*, February 22, 2007.

Scott Jaschik, "An Honest Conversation About Alcohol," *Inside Higher Ed*, February 16, 2007.

Kathiann M. Kowalski, "Alcohol: A Real Threat," *Current Health 2: A Weekly Reader*, December 2003.

Bill McKelway, "How Kids Can Drink at Home, Legally: Va. Muddles Message, Some Say, by Letting Parents Serve at Home," *Richmond Times-Dispatch*, January 28, 2007.

Jacqueline W. Miller, Timothy S. Naimi, Robert D. Brewer, and Sherry Everett Jones, "Binge Drinking and Associated Health Risk Behaviors Among High School Students," *Pediatrics*, January 2007.

Ted R. Miller, David T. Levy, Rebecca S. Spicer, and Dexter M. Taylor, "Societal Costs of Underage Drinking," *Journal of Studies on Alcohol*, July 2006.

Jon P. Nelson, "Advertising, Alcohol, and Youth: Is the Alcoholic Beverage Industry Targeting Minors with Magazine Ads?" *Regulation*, Summer 2005.

Vanessa O'Connell, "Uneasy Compromise: To Keep Teens Safe, Some Parents Allow Drinking at Home," *Wall Street Journal*, September 14, 2004.

Michele Oreckin, "You Must Be Over 21 to Drink in This Living Room: A Crackdown on House Parties Stirs Up a Debate About Privacy," *Time*, April 18, 2005.

John Ritter, "Laws Crash Underage Drinking Parties," *USA Today*, January 5, 2007.

Sandy Fertman Ryan, "Wasted Lives: The Truth About Teen Girls and Drinking, *Girls' Life*, October–November 2004.

John R. Wilke and Christopher Lawton, "Amid Fight Over Teen Drinking, Panel Weighs New Tax on Alcohol," *Wall Street Journal*, July 11, 2003.

Internet Source

Office of Juvenile Justice and Delinquency Prevention, *Drinking In America: Myths, Realities, and Prevention Policy*, August 2005. www.udetc.org/publications.htm.

Web Sites

Alcohol: Problems and Solutions (www2.potsdam.edu/hansondj). This Web site contains numerous articles about alcohol, written from a variety of perspectives. The site also offers facts, links to other Web sites, and references for further research.

College Drinking: Changing the Culture (www.collegedrinking-prevention.gov). This Web site, created by the National Institute on Alcohol Abuse and Alcoholism, is a resource for research-based information on issues related to alcohol abuse and binge drinking among college students.

The Cool Spot: The Young Teen's Place for Info on Alcohol and Resisting Peer Pressure (www.thecoolspot.gov). The Cool Spot was created for kids eleven to thirteen years old by the National Institute on Alcohol Abuse and Alcoholism. The Web site offers facts about alcohol, quizzes, and tools for resisting peer pressure.

Stop Underage Drinking: Portal of Federal Resources (www .stopalcoholabuse.gov). This Web site is a portal to a range of government-approved materials on underage drinking. It offers links to agency sites and includes a catalog of related federal programs.

INDEX

PICTURE CREDITS

All photos © AP Images